The Roots that Clutch

To Zena —

May these letters be a good
impulse to getting lost in thought!

Fr. Thomas

The Roots that Clutch

Letters on the Origins of Things

Thomas Esposito

WIPF & STOCK · Eugene, Oregon

THE ROOTS THAT CLUTCH
Letters on the Origins of Things

Wipf & Stock
An Imprint of Wipf and Stock Publishers
199 W. 8th Ave., Suite 3
Eugene, OR 97401

www.wipfandstock.com

PAPERBACK ISBN: 978-1-5326-4486-3
HARDCOVER ISBN: 978-1-5326-4487-0
EBOOK ISBN: 978-1-5326-4488-7

Manufactured in the U.S.A.

Contents

Acknowledgments

I WISH TO EXPRESS my gratitude to several confreres, friends, and students who aided me in the crafting of this volume. My fellow Cistercian Fr. Roch Kereszty, a self-proclaimed gadfly, pleasantly and persistently nagged me to share these letters with him as I composed them. I received valuable editorial suggestions from my Abbot, Fr. Peter Verhalen, and I am thankful for his support of this work. In addition, I enjoyed happy collaborations with many former and current students of mine at the University of Dallas. I extend particular shout-outs (or shouts-out?) of gratitude to Alec, Finbar (now Br. Christopher in my community), Teresa, and Kitty. To them, and to my future students, this book is dedicated.

A special note of appreciation goes to Jacquelyn Lee, who volunteered her excellent editorial skills in laboring strenuously but (she tells me) happily during term paper and final exam season to improve these letters.

Notes:
Earlier versions of the letters to Jonathan, Barnabas, Dr. Seuss, and Galadriel were published in *The Texas Catholic*, the newspaper of the Diocese of Dallas. Special thanks go to Michael Gresham for his permission to print them here in a new, lettered form.

All translations from the Bible are my own.

To the Reader

Dear Reader,

You may not be a fan of poetry, but I want to tell you about a delightful poem I have long admired. The poem is entitled "Digging," and in short and simple verses the great Irishman Seamus Heaney fondly presents his recollections of the gardening his father and grandfather loved to do. He visualizes the spade sinking "into gravelly ground," his father "stooping in rhythm" as he digs in flower beds and potato patches. He boasts of his grandfather's legendary ability to cut turf, and recalls the smells and sensations of his own handling of potatoes and "soggy peat." All of this comes to him in the form of memories, as "living roots awaken in my head."[1]

Rather than take up that same generational trade, though, Heaney regards his pen as his humble instrument of choice, claiming he has "no spade to follow men like them. / Between my finger and my thumb / The squat pen rests. / I'll dig with it." It is with his poetic pen, rather than his father's tools, that Heaney hopes to break up the earth of the soul, and plant new seeds in the heart-soil of his readers. He accomplishes this in "Digging" by allowing his memories of family and farming to fertilize the seedbed of his lyrical mind. The poet, in other words, plunges the spade of his pen into the nourishing ground of his past, and that literary gardening yields a harvest of graced nourishment for his readers.

Have you ever pondered how marvelous roots are? Those of trees shoot downward, lunging slowly but firmly into the brown earth where they usually remain hidden from human eyes. Beneath the ground, they strengthen the visible trunk and branches, suck nutrients from the soil, and channel water to generate growth. I have heard that the intricate root system of a tree grows as wide and deep below as the width and height of the

---

1. Heaney, "Digging," 3–4.

branches that stretch skyward. What we see from our earthen vantage point is mirrored, though undetected, beneath our feet.

The lotus flower pitches its roots in water rather than soil. Its leaves float gently on the water's surface, and hold aloft a beautiful flower of colored petals. The physical characteristics of the lotus are the inspiration for its symbolic meaning in the great religions of Asia, especially Hinduism and Buddhism: the flower, escaping the illusory and murky world of sense experience represented by water, emerges above it, and opens itself to the world of union and contemplation symbolized by the limitless sky. In imitation of the transcendent flower, the lotus position is the basic starting point for yoga meditation in these Eastern traditions.

Just as the physical yields to the symbolic in the case of the lotus flower, so also are the roots of trees and plants employed in a variety of metaphorical ways. When individuals in the United States trace their ancestral lineage by means of a family tree, they often speak of their genealogical roots lying in the lands from which their ancestors emigrated. The study of language often features the concept of root letters, or consonants forming the foundation of nouns and verbs. The verb systems of Semitic languages such as Hebrew and Arabic are arranged according to a tri-literal root, meaning the basic structure of the verb is composed of three consonants around which prefixes and suffixes are added to create new words and shades of meaning. A religion such as Christianity, or a country such as India, possesses roots deeply embedded in a particular region, stretching for millennia into the soil of history. Whether doctrines or practices, dominant figures or defining historical events, the roots of a given religion, people, or nation nourish those living in the present with the sustenance of prior generations and traditions.

To bring Heaney's poem and my musings on roots together, the book you are currently holding is the fruit of my own digging within myself to examine the roots and experiences which have formed me and nourished my thinking, praying, and being. In my previous epistolary collection, entitled *Letters of Fire*, I explain my indebtedness to T. S. Eliot for much of my early intellectual growth and enduring spiritual insight, and this present book of letters falls under his aegis once more.[2] The title of this volume comes from lines 19–24 of his grand, strange, and immensely difficult poem "The Waste Land":

2. Esposito, *Letters of Fire*, xi–xii.

What are the roots that clutch, what branches grow
Out of this stony rubbish? Son of man,
You cannot say, or guess, for you know only
A heap of broken images, where the sun beats,
And the dead tree gives no shelter, the cricket no relief,
And the dry stone no sound of water.[3]

Eliot's poem, penned in the aftermath of the First World War, portrays with an odd and cold starkness the desiccated wilderness of European lands and culture. On the surface of that "stony rubbish" that once was a grand civilization, the poet sees only shattered mirrors, "a heap of broken images," an unrelenting waste land of howling desert. Whatever roots had nurtured the trees of religion and government and Western culture were now shriveled and naked, senselessly standing sentinel after so many torrents of destruction had devastated them. Eliot presents his jarring poem, full of sentence fragments and obscure literary references, as a reflection of the world he lives in, one in which the roots no longer support the trunk and branches of religion and civilization. The reader gets the nostalgically tragic sense that nothing from the past but fragments, presented as barren roots lacking any vitality, can be salvaged.

It is tempting to think the same of the world we inhabit today. The daily channeling of violence in the name of religion or ethnic strife, the worldwide uncertainty of a hopeful future for the next generation, the frequent (if only fleeting) triumph of ideologies of greed and repression, all contribute to the malaise which Eliot so acutely diagnosed in "The Waste Land." If I may liken the Christian faith and the culture produced by that faith to a tree, its roots have been exposed for some time in the West due to a growing hostility to the supernatural. The desire of many secularist politicians is to see those roots wither, or even actively work to eradicate them. Eliot's poem lends itself quite nicely to such a dire assessment of both secular and Christian culture.

But I refuse to succumb to such a temptation, however alluring and even comforting it often seems, and these letters explain why. Instead of transferring the plant to entirely new soil in which the roots can sink into more welcoming and fertile earth (whatever that might mean practically), I would rather do as Heaney does: make history and memories, however good or tinged with evil they might be, bear good fruit in the present and

3. Eliot, *The Complete Poems and Plays*, 38.

for the future. Each letter in this collection began, you might say, as a seed in my own soul. My aim was to analyze the roots that plunge into the fertile ground of my imagination. I am firmly convinced that my own Christian intellectual and cultural heritage has a vitalizing sap to channel to the men and women of the twenty-first century, whose hearts were made by a sower who scatters good seed. This desire to find what remains and make it grow again is a fundamental trait of Jewish and Christian faith.

You may very well think that a book of letters is a ridiculous way of pondering the origins of things and responding to the gigantic human failings and challenges of our time. I have no trouble imagining that a collection of epistles to an eclectic cast of personages, most of them dead or fictional, could strike you as downright absurd and not worth your while. Yet I find that such a format offers a uniquely refreshing perspective on the source of many realities, whether personal, cultural, or religious. In *Letters of Fire*, I drew inspiration from another T.S. Eliot poem, "Little Gidding" from *Four Quartets*, in which the poet observes the ability of the living to conduct a salutary conversation with the dead, a communication "tongued with fire beyond the language of the living."[4] The creation of an illuminating correspondence with deceased historical characters and literary figures, to change metaphors from one book to the next, puts down new roots in fresh soil, and can even vivify hopes long since dried up by despair or ignorance.

To be honest, I had no central theme unifying the letters in the first book, aside from my dilettantish love of learning. In both works, my focus is catholic in the small c sense: embracing, talking to, and sharing with anyone and everyone. Dialogue with the dead, I have found, is a strangely fruitful and vivifying enterprise! The specific concept of roots, though, gives a greater unity to the individual letters of this volume.

Many different meanings of roots and origins will overlap in the following pages. Some names of my addressees will be immediately familiar to you, but I am certain you have never heard of Captain James Harvey, or Fr. Aloysius Kimecz. My letters to these two men are part of a digging into the field of my own life: the former is a blood relative with roots stretching back to Ireland and Civil War-era Philadelphia, the latter a confrere and friend in the Cistercian Abbey I now call home. I did not devote much overt attention to the monastic aspect of my life in *Letters of Fire*, and the bookends of this new epistolary tome offer reflections on monk life and the inspiration that guides men and women to this radical way of serving God. St. Benedict

4. Ibid., 139.

and Taylor Swift (yes, you read that right) set the tone at the beginning, and two twentieth-century Cistercians who suffered horribly at the hands of the Communist regime in Hungary—Abbot Wendelin Endrédy and Fr. Aloysius—at the end.

Rather than tell you a story about where things like sin and egos and Punxsutawney Phil come from, I enlist the help of people who have better insight about some part of the human condition than myself. Eve, that ill-fated and maltreated mother of all the living, gets a new hearing in my analysis of Genesis 3 and its explanation of the perennial reality of sin and death (spoiler alert: Adam is just as culpable as the first woman!). Miss Havisham, one of the most haunting characters ever created by Mr. Charles Dickens, is the object of my musings on anger and its chilling effect on the human heart, created to be a hearth radiating merciful warmth. The earth itself is the focus of my letter to the two peasants posing in a beautiful painting by Jean-François Millet entitled *The Angelus*. The beloved Dr. Seuss presumably will not take my letter to him kindly, since I castigate him for making millions of children think they are almighty Pelagians and the sole protagonists in their own super-duper-special universe. If you don't know what a Pelagian is, you will after perusing that letter, and then hopefully you will understand why *Oh! The Places You'll Go!* encourages its readers to become selfish ego-monsters. To Kisa Gotami, an early follower of the Buddha, I ask how her understanding of perennial questions about suffering and the self harmonize with or differ from my own Christian perspective.

Seeds are a primary topic of my letter to Heraclitus, a philosopher who lived centuries before Jesus. I get him up to speed on the work of the Christian philosophers St. John and St. Justin Martyr, who both wrote about the same idea of *logos* found in the extant fragments of his works that have come down to us. St. John defines the *logos*, which we usually render as "word" in English, as the person Jesus Christ, and St. Justin Martyr asserts that Greek philosophers such as Heraclitus possessed *logoi spermatikoi*, or seeds of the word, even before the time of Christ. What this means is that partial truths or insights about God and beauty and happiness may be gleaned in fields outside the confines of the Christian faith, and can even help us come to comprehend the infinite majesty of God and the gift of Christ to all human hearts longing for the full breadth of the *Logos*.

Not all seeds sown in the human heart, however, are healthy or life-giving. In some of these letters, I unearth the roots of current social maladies, especially in my beloved United States of America. In the letters to

Martin Luther King Jr. and Roberto Clemente, I lament the racism that continues to ruin lives and cripple relationships between blacks, whites, and Hispanics in my country. Poor Alexander Graham Bell, the inventor of the telephone, stands on the wrong end of a rant about how his brainchild, the cell phone, has become the source of undeniable social regress and the stupidification of those caught in its screeny thrall. Lyle Alzado, a football lineman convinced that his steroid use killed him, is the recipient of a meditation on the crazed lust for athletic glory and the lack of restraint in the human will. The origins of greed are the object of my reminiscence to Nike, the goddess of victory and patron of the shoe and clothing empire today, about a humorous incident from my days as an impulsive child.

Sprinkled in the midst of such letters are others dedicated to topics of spirituality and faith. Several biblical characters who have always fascinated me get some unexpected fan mail, such as the sinful woman from Luke 7, Barabbas, and Barnabas. Saints and heroes of mine—most notably Benedict, Thomas More (my namesake in religion), and Bernadette—deserve special mention. Having set foot on the streets of Jerusalem, I wanted to pen a letter to the holy city to clarify my own thoughts on the possibility of peace in this world. The concluding letter to Galadriel, the beautiful elven lady from *The Lord of the Rings*, is a testimony to hope and graceful fortitude. I think the tone and content of that final note, one of "hope without guarantees," express the essence of my intention with this collection.

And so, good reader, I invite you to think of these pages as seeds of the *Logos* which I wish to scatter in the fertile soil of your mind and heart. They have fallen onto paper from the tree of my mind, and contain the genetic material of my own personality, history, beliefs, and sense of humor. If given proper watering and cultivation by you in the form of reading and perhaps even praying about them, I hope you will observe them grow, and perhaps even sprout roots and furnish you with vitalizing intellectual and spiritual nutrients. If they don't accomplish this admittedly grandiose purpose, at least I can take comfort knowing that I did a little digging in the garden of my soul, and harvested much fruit for myself in the process.

God bless,
Fr. Thomas

Saint Benedict[1]

To my dear abbot, *gratia Benedictus et nomine,*

Please consider me a son who has listened to his father's instructions for a mere decade, and has tried, with small success, to incline the ear of his heart to them. What I cannot show by obedient actions, I can attempt to express in gratitude through these poor but fervent words. The centuries separating us have vindicated your wisdom and faithful insight, both of which are timeless because they guide time-bound souls to the eternal God. A desire to inquire deeper into your monastic wisdom has prompted me to write you today.

In your *Rule*, you regard the gyrovague monk, always restless and bound to no permanent home, as the most wretched creature on earth. I often think of the possible scorn you would heap on me for my frequent travels. When I joined my monastery, I did not foresee the great amount of roaming I would have the privilege to undertake (always with my abbot's permission, of course!). In fact, I like to joke that I made my vow of stability on an airplane 30,000 feet above land (though considering your disposition against boisterous laughter, I doubt you would approve of such frivolity)!

I can assure you that I have but one monastic home to which I happily return after each voyage, but I have spent a significant amount of time outside the cloistered paradise of my abbey in Texas. I do not apologize for my travels, though, because among the myriad blessings I have received

---

1. Saint Benedict of Norcia (ca. AD 480–ca. 540) lived as a hermit for a short time before establishing a cenobitic community of monks at Monte Cassino in Italy. He is considered the founder of Western monasticism, and his *Rule* is still the governing document of many monastic orders, including the Benedictines and Cistercians. He is also one of the patron saints of Europe. The opening greeting is a play on his name: *Benedictus* in Latin means "blessed," and therefore he is "blessed in grace and in name."

as a Cistercian monk on the go, standing in the places you graced with your presence rank among the highest. I have scaled the massive heights of Monte Cassino on multiple occasions, climbing switchbacks to venerate your mortal remains, as well as those of your sister, Saint Scholastica, who is buried next to you.

Almost 1,500 years after your death, the monks living there were forced to flee as the Nazi army took command of the majestic mountain on which the abbey stands. The American army, trying to reach Rome from the south, bombed the monastery to heaps of rubble in March of 1944, thinking that the Germans still occupied it. The dreaded Nazis had, in fact, evacuated just before the shelling began. Sadly, the church and monastic cells were pummeled and destroyed. Only the crypt, containing your remains and those of Scholastica, emerged intact.

Fortunately, the Americans eventually seized Rome, and the Allied forces gradually secured a total triumph over the Nazi regime in Europe. Thanks to the Marshall Plan, a strategic effort to rebuild the continent ravaged by war, Monte Cassino was restored to its former glory; the cornerstone of the reconstructed church has "1949 AD" inscribed on it. I once went on a tour of the grounds with a group of Cistercians from various parts of the globe. When the guide described the Allied bombing of Monte Cassino, everyone glared at me, the lone American, with mostly feigned anger. But one elderly Italian woman with sharp elbows nudged me and shoved a picture book depicting the devastation under my nose. Her face was contorted into an accusatory snarl; I translated her menacing glance as, "Look whatchya did, ya little jerk!" Sheer charity prevented me from reminding her to be grateful that she spoke Italian and not German.

This is not, however, the only Benedictine rebuilding project I wish to share with you.

Monte Cassino is undoubtedly a glorious and sacred place. It is a city set on a hill, and its white stones transmit inspired light to all who pass by. You finished writing your *Rule* for monks while guiding the community there as abbot during the last years of your life. My favorite place to follow in your footsteps, though, is the cave where you first found refuge from the noise and distraction of the world. The bus ride to Subiaco, east of Rome, takes about 80 minutes, and ends at the foot of the modern town. I always brought at least one fellow monk along with me when I visited. My confreres and I would amble up the gradual road to the base of the mountain where you made your first retreat from the world. The climb to Sacro Speco, your holy cave, is shortened by a rocky trail leading more directly upward than the winding road used by automobiles. Your humble cave was eventually engulfed by a modest monastery and church complex, but the silence you craved is still available today, in spite of frequent tourists and pilgrims.

I must point out a humorous example of the rivalry amongst your spiritual sons, one enshrined in the church above Sacro Speco. You have heard from the heavenly newsroom, I presume, that your Benedictine Order became rich and lax in the centuries following your death, and was reformed in the twelfth century by a group of men who came to be called Cistercians. One of the Benedictine monks decorating the Subiaco church in the fourteenth or fifteenth century got the brilliant idea to portray the enmity between his Order and the renegade reformers in paint. In the frescoes depicting scenes from your life lining the main nave of the church, that artist-monk put the black-and-white Cistercian habit on the wicked monks who tried to poison you. The distracted monk pulled out of choir by the devil also sports those same robes. The proud Cistercian in me objects to the roguish treatment we received at the hands of your black-robed children, not to mention the anachronism of Cistercians living during your lifetime!

My favorite spot in Subiaco stands below Sacro Speco, about halfway between your cave and the gorgeous waterfall and lagoon where you obtained water. A complex of ruined brick buildings lies beside the road. According to tradition, this was originally the site of Emperor Nero's summer estate—the same Nero who unleashed a vicious persecution of Christians by scapegoating them for the fire which ravaged Rome in AD 64. By the time you arrived on the historical scene in the early sixth century, the place had been abandoned for many years. The story goes that when you began to attract disciples to share your solitary life, you realized that you would have to relinquish the peace of Sacro Speco, and a larger communal home needed to be found. You apparently did not search very far for such a place—you and your first followers inhabited the remains of Nero's house, and requisitioned it for your prayerful purposes.

The magnitude of that historical fact struck me quite powerfully as I stood before those brick fragments. It prompted me to compose a poem when I returned to Rome that day. Though poor in form, it is rich in the zeal I tried to channel for your monastic house. The first part of the poem, which I simply titled "Subiaco," treats of your moving in and the gradual explosion of monastic life inspired by your example:

The man of God removed himself once more.
The world was lost, now Sacro Speco too;
His dwelling with himself could not be kept
A secret light submerged in silent caves.
He took his heart, a bursting flame, and stood
Above; not far below, he found a heap
Which Nero, devil's fire, once had called
His home and court in summertime retreat.
The man went there with other burning souls
Who built a school and torched the place with prayer.
How strange that one man's blazing should ignite
A thousand matches striking pagan lands
With silent flint and scores of kindled monks
Who stoked this ember red in Caesar's house.

The thought of you praying in Nero's estate still captivates me, reverend father. A singular grace is available to those privileged to tread where saints have walked, built, and prayed, and I am particularly fascinated by the fact that you appropriated the relics of a pagan emperor for your own use. Were you aware that the previous tenant of those walled rooms was a martyr-maker of your fellow Christians? Did you ponder the beautiful irony of occupying his territory for the noble purposes of Christian prayer, long after he had gone violently to his grave? But you soon outgrew that space as well, due to the number of monks entrusting themselves to your care, and you migrated south to Monte Cassino, the hill that would henceforth be the heart of Benedictine life.

Your presence in Nero's house, dear abbot, is a timely image for me to ponder as I survey the society around me today. An eerily similar sort of occupation is occurring in many parts of the previously Christian world. I have heard in recent years of glorious churches, built with the intent of magnifying the Lord and housing the presence of the bread of life, being sold on account of the shrinking number of parishioners engaged in the liturgy and Christian way of life. On your own European continent, the citizens of old Christian strongholds such as England, Germany, and the Netherlands have yielded, rapidly and shockingly, to a worldview that has absolutely no interest in matters supernatural. On the contrary, opportunists have seized upon the idea of purchasing empty churches and transforming them into everyday enterprises: from pizzerias with the main oven strategically placed on the very spot where the altar once stood, to discotheques, cafés, and bookstores, many ornate cathedrals have been reformatted to promote brazenly secular ends.

The fate of these churches linked up in my mind with your requisition of Nero's ruins, and the contrast between them provided me with inspiration for the second part of my poem:

> A nameless girl is whirled and tossed across
> The space which once held pews for kneeling prayer.
> As smoke and lusty steam like incense rise
> Above the mass to stain the Gothic stone,
> Orgasmic bombs are dropped from organ pipes
> While stain'd glass sleeps amid the darkened din.
> A pizzeria down the street now stands
> Where schoolboys used to serve at morning Mass;
> Upon the spot where bread was once made flesh
> A forno sits and heats the pizza pies;
> These feed the hungry mouths who like the charm
> Of feasting in the empty space of faith.
> The baker raises dough above his head
> And winks at Jesus, statued in the niche.

The renovation of sacred places is simply a symptom of a sobering fact: the Christian faith, and the vestiges reminding us of a past rooted in it, are disappearing at an alarming rate. That Jesus himself foresaw such a situation is hardly consoling; his question, "When the Son of Man comes, will he find faith on the earth?" (Luke 18:8), does not receive an answer.

What is a Christian to do in the face of such spite against the Spirit and anything associated with it, whether unconscious or aggressive? Just as you escaped the worldly snares of Rome and found refuge in a secluded life of prayer, St. Benedict, many Christians today are advocating a similar retreat from a post-Christian society, whether in Europe or the United States. Your life is hailed as an example to be imitated, but now by entire families and parishes. Just as your monastic revolution saved Western civilization during a time of crisis, so today many are crying out for a "Benedict option" of withdrawal from the world. The phrase has received a variety of interpretations. Some claim that small but creative pockets of Christians must break away from public society and move underground, in order to prevent the flame of the Christian faith from being extinguished by rampaging secular winds.

The comparison, dear abbot, is both apt and tempting. The very expression used to describe the retreat of the first desert hermits from the world, *fuga mundi* (flight from the world), springs naturally to mind in this context. Some people might even assert that monks such as myself have already abandoned the world to its own devices by taking refuge inside a monastery, safe from the slings and arrows of outrageous indifference and even vicious ideologies. Enflamed by Maccabean-style zeal for our traditions, we would be idealists bent on saving our precious pearls from the trampling of secular swine!

Yet I do not regard my own vocation in those terms, and I would urge caution on those who think that a mass exodus of Christians from public life is necessary to safeguard the faith for future generations. In appealing to your own withdrawal from the world as inspiration during this present crisis, many fail to understand that you did not intend to save Western civilization by living in a cave and forming monastic communities. You simply responded to an alluring call from God to dwell with yourself and by yourself in solitude, and in so doing you created a new form of life which became the bastion of Western civilization. I might call your withdrawal a happenstance event were it not clearly impressed by the fingerprints of providence. Rather than regard your move to the cave as a template for modern-day Christians, I would highlight how your way of life subtly traced out a solution to the pressing needs of your time. It is in this sense, I believe, that a philosopher, Alasdair MacIntyre, wrote of the urgency of a new St. Benedict for our day.[2]

My hunch, holy abbot, is that a widespread running for the hills is not a prudent move for most followers of Christ. It risks quieting the voice that people in the world, ignorant but still human *and therefore open to the divine*, desperately need to hear. While cold ignorance or open hostility can easily dismay even the most courageous of Christians, the words of the ancient "Letter to Diognetus" are resoundingly clear regarding the necessity of the Christian presence in the world: "What the soul is in the body, Christians are in the world . . . The soul dwells in the body, but does not belong to the body, and Christians dwell in the world, but do not belong to the world."[3]

2. MacIntyre, *After Virtue*, 263.
3. "Letter to Diognetus." In Richardson, *Early Christian Fathers*, 218.

Am I thereby condemning monastic life, or claiming that monks and nuns have abdicated their responsibility to be the animating principle of a society ignorant of God? I don't believe so, and I think you would agree with me. In my view, abbot Benedict, monasteries have a definite and essential role to play in the life not only of the church, but also of those Christians living and praying in this post-Christian world.

In chapter 53 of your *Rule*, you instruct your monks to regard guests arriving at the monastery as Christ himself.[4] Most translations state that all "hospitality" or "goodness" should be shown to visitors; the actual Latin word you employ, however, is *humanitas*. The *humanitas* we monks must display to our guests startles me in connection with the topic I have been writing about. I regard my monastery, and ideally all monasteries, as refreshing oases of culture, where a weary soul may be rejuvenated by the quiet spaces, liturgical chants, and calm hope offered by the monks. If you would permit me to expand the meaning of your term "guests" to include all searchers for truth, and even the whole world, I think your injunction of *humanitas* can be an animating lifeline for all people, whether fervent Christians or secular seekers.

What do I have in mind? Only a tiny portion of men and women are called to dedicate themselves to the Lord in religious life. These have the humbling privilege of channeling the waters of wisdom and faith that nourish them in their monastic oasis to thirsty travelers, images of God who are disoriented by the mirages of happiness and hope which compose the world. Our *humanitas* is what we have been blessed by God to receive: the goodness of a mind capable of recognizing the imprint of its Creator, and a heart able to love someone other and greater than itself. The guests of our monasteries are seeking a retreat from an increasingly inhumane world which denies that beautiful link between creature and Creator, and they need to be reminded of their natural desire "to long for life, and to see good things" (Ps 34:13). What a monastery can provide such seekers, I think, is a refreshing way to approach their work within a world created good but distorted by sin and selfishness. Perhaps in the course of our liturgy, our learning, and our prayer, we can point them to the ruins of Nero's house which need to be occupied by Christians and transformed into "schools for the Lord's service" (from the prologue of the *Rule*).[5] The world needs such souls to remind it of something more glorious than ego-centered feelings

---

4. Fry, *Rule of St. Benedict*, 258–59.

5. Ibid., 164–65.

and fleeting pleasures; those souls, in turn, need to be supported as they face battering and hostile winds.

The value of a monastery for the broader culture certainly extends beyond its *humanitas* and hospitality. The medieval monasteries served to domesticate the barbarian hordes with agricultural techniques. Your monks preserved the great ideas of pagan and Christian culture through the copying of manuscripts, which were often works of stunning artistic genius. Their life of work and prayer, as the title of Jean Leclercq's famous book illustrates, harmonized "the love of learning and the desire for God."[6] The unparalleled beauty of Gregorian chant—taking its name from St. Gregory the Great, your biographer—unites angelic psalms and human voices, and even today calms souls listening with the ear of their heart. As Gregory's successor, Pope Benedict XVI, said so eloquently in a speech during his 2008 visit to the former Cistercian house of studies in Paris,

> The monastery serves *eruditio*, the formation and education of man—a formation whose ultimate aim is that man should learn how to serve God. But it also includes the formation of reason—education—through which man learns to perceive, in the midst of words, the Word itself.[7]

From our monasteries, that word, studied and contemplated in *lectio divina*, should be dispersed through spiritual direction, education of the young, and writings.

Despite my biased hope that monasticism can contribute to the rebuilding of a more Christian (and therefore more human) culture, holy father Benedict, I have no rosy illusions about the future of American and Western civilization. The final section of my "Subiaco" poem reflects a certain pessimism of mine regarding our secular culture:

> Tomorrow boasts of godlessness and ghosts
> Which walk in mem'ried quarters, telling tales
> In ruined stone, in silent bells, in church;
> And we alone are left as reliqued souls
> To note the setting suns and Christian shades.
> But must we make our graves of hallowed space,
> Exchanging fire for frost, the pearl for dust?
> For I am not a dying man, not yet,

6. See Leclercq, *The Love of Learning and the Desire for God*, 1–7.

7. Benedict XVI, "Meeting with Representatives from the World of Culture," para. 3.

And we have stood, still stand, on living ground,
Convinced, with proof, that death can yield a dawn
And Love still dares to sow in arid earth.
When places pass, and hearts aflame grow cold,
Please grant us *now* a faith begot of hope,
Assured that we have not believed in vain.

I wrote those lines several years ago, before I came to think of *humanitas* as the great gift monasticism can offer souls ignorant of their own glorious humanity. They present a bleaker outlook than the one I hold now, but their sobering perspective is still instructive. Christians must not abandon their ship to the stormy waves simply because they cannot control the winds or waters, and I consider monasticism a rudder steering the ship of the church (indeed, of all humanity) on a Godward course. I take very seriously my privileged duty to share with our guests, and channel to others through them, the rivers of living water which I have found in my monastery. Saint Gregory the Great wrote that you once received a singular grace in contemplation: the whole world was presented before your eyes as if it were collected in a single ray of the sun. May your illuminating example and powerful prayers intercede for me, and all the monks and nuns living under your patronage, that we might be faithful collectors of your inspiring rays and refreshing aqueducts to all who come to us seeking God.

Saint Thomas More[1]

To SAINT THOMAS MORE, the king's good servant, and God's first:

Above my desk is a print of your silhouette, taken from the famous Holbein portrait, set against the text of one of your prison letters to your daughter Meg. A monastic confrere of mine created it for me, and I have placed it in my university office to guard and guide me in my work. Gazing at it now, the thought of penning some scribbled musings to you strikes me as silly. I have often succumbed to the temptation to write nothing at all to you, rather than organize a vast array of half-baked inspirations arising from your life and writings. With much hesitation, then, do I address myself to you, a man so eminently endowed with that rare combination of learning, humor, and holiness. Given your delight at the fact that your last name means "foolishness" in Greek, you would likely chuckle as you chide me for flattering you at the outset of this letter. How can I properly express my debt to your intellectual genius and "good mother wit?"[2] What is the proper way for me to thank you for your witness of faith against tyranny, and your courage in the face of martyrdom? And how can I worthily receive the inheritance which you, my patron saint, have bequeathed to me, and which I have so often neglected?

Perhaps the best place to begin is my own acquaintance with your legacy, both secular and sacred. I take as my starting point a verse from the pen of Saint Paul, who encouraged the Corinthians, "Be imitators of me as

---

1. Saint Thomas More (1477–1535) was an English lawyer, writer, husband, father, Renaissance humanist, and theologian. He rose to the rank of Lord Chancellor under King Henry VIII. After refusing to swear the Oath of Supremacy and therefore acknowledge Henry as Supreme Head of the Church of England, More was executed. The Catholic Church venerates him as a martyr. Among his best known writings are *Utopia* and *The Sadness of Christ*.

2. More, *A Dialogue Concerning Heresies*, 132.

I am of Christ" (1 Cor 11:1). If to imitate a saint is to imitate Christ, then you have made me more like our Lord than I ever could have hoped to be without your example. To be sure, I have not imitated you to the letter. My desire to be a lawyer irretrievably evaporated in high school thanks to a nauseatingly boring summer at a law firm. Nor have I followed your footsteps as a husband and father. On this score, it may seem strange that a monk vowed to celibacy should take as his patron a lawyer, statesman, and family man. Yet I consider your sponsorship of my monastic and priestly life an immense and altogether appropriate gift.

Your own discernment as a young man greatly helped me in my youth, particularly as I wrestled with a vocation to the abbey I now call home. While engaged in your legal studies, you resided with Carthusian monks, praying with them as your studies allowed and pondering your own future. You either uttered or wrote down a phrase which I found quite comforting as I grew increasingly agitated with my own discernment of the Lord's will for my life. You feared that you would be a "licentious priest," and determined instead that you would be capable of being "a chaste husband."[3] The ways of providence guided me to the same terms, but the opposite conclusion: I was made to be, by the grace of God, a chaste priest rather than a licentious husband.

But your discernment was simply one of many aspects that drew me to you. In requesting to adopt the name Thomas as my own to symbolize my new life as a monk, I looked to you as my model. My abbot was good enough to grant me the name Thomas, thus equipping my monastic community with a novel but powerful intercessor. I was attracted to your humor and humanism, by which you manifested the full glory of the human being alive in God, whether through secular politics, religious devotion, or pranks on your family and friends. I have pondered what a privilege it must have been to be a guest in your home at Chelsea. The accounts of your dinners and evening entertainment are filled with delightful memories of music, laughter, poetry, hearty banter, and shenanigans done by the family pet monkey. Your children would have shamed me in a Latin contest, but I would have made a great effort to prove to you that my learning was not half lame. I would then have challenged you to prove the same! I have always envied your dear colleague Erasmus, who noted that you were a natural friend to all, indeed one "born for friendship"[4]—what a treasure it would have been to know you in the flesh!

3. Wegemer, *A Portrait of Courage*, 11.
4. See Wegemer and Smith, *A Thomas More Source Book*, 6.

You would not be surprised, I suppose, that your legacy was largely forgotten for several hundred years in the church you loved following your death. To that bit of news, I imagine you quipping something to the effect that losing one's head generally indicates a lack of popularity! Fortunately, the Catholic Church did eventually canonize you, though the event took place a full 400 years after your martyrdom.

You would surely be tickled to know that in 2010, the bishop of Rome—whose authority you so ardently defended by your writing and then by your silence—set foot in the very Westminster Hall where you were convicted of high treason. Quite early in his brilliant discourse, the Holy Father specifically invoked you as he reminded his listeners of the need for a "profound and ongoing dialogue" between "secular rationality and religious belief" in the political and legislative dimensions of society.[5] The historical irony of Pope Benedict XVI standing on the same stones that heard your death sentence was at once so wondrous and strange that you surely would have commemorated it with a joke at your own expense, or perhaps an epigram on the value of patience. The papists may yet reclaim England!

Just a few years before your canonization in 1935, G. K. Chesterton, a fellow Englishman, wrote the following about you: "Blessed Thomas More is more important at this moment than at any moment since his death, even perhaps the great moment of his dying; but he is not quite so important as he will be in about a hundred years' time."[6] In my experience of reading Chesterton, I find that I vehemently disagree with him after a first reading, consider him too much of a cute sophist to be taken seriously after a second, and entirely agree with him on the third.

But just why he is right regarding your importance to my own time is not easy to pinpoint. Your courageous stand for the truths of both "Rome and reason," as Chesterton put it, is perhaps what he had foremost in mind.[7] And indeed, Chesterton presciently foresaw the inevitable advance of "enlightened" thought entirely hostile to the Christian faith. This euphemistic phrase is a mere mask for an ideology manifesting itself in increasingly open and alarming ways. Several years ago, Pope Benedict XVI summed

---

5. Pope Benedict XVI, "Meeting with the Representatives of British Society including the Diplomatic Corps, Politicians, Academics, and Business Leaders," para. 6.

6. Chesterton, "A Turning Point in History," In *The Fame of Blessed Thomas More*, 63–64.

7. Ibid., 64.

up this dominant way of thinking as "the dictatorship of relativism."[8] The obvious temptation for an admirer of your witness to the church and the natural law is to liken our generation to yours, and worry that such an end as you suffered is soon to befall us, even if the martyrdom be white rather than red.

Yet that line of interpretation glosses over, I think, the more profound gift you offer to the women and men of today. In a sense, I lament the manner in which you are remembered. Your joyful family life, the legendary education of your children, and your brilliant work which ushered in the Renaissance of letters have all been upstaged, and inevitably so, by your heroic witness of courage and conscience. I am certainly grateful, nevertheless, that such a witness is available to us, however costly it was to yourself and your country. I think the most precious inheritance Catholics can receive from you today, especially those under your patronage, is the manner in which you readied yourself for the supreme moment of your witness. Your prayer-prepared courage, generated and stored over the course of an immensely blessed life, is most beautifully portrayed in your meditations entitled *The Sadness of Christ*.

Your choice of Scripture to ponder at the end of your life is easy enough to understand. The thought of you poring over the sequence of Jesus' agony in the garden, his betrayal, and the beginning of his trial *while enduring an identical agony*, bestows a great solemnity on your text. The beginning of Jesus' passion narrative was the mirror in which you regarded your own passion, and I cannot imagine the loneliness you must have experienced as you entered into the same destiny as our Lord. How incredibly graced, though, is the good which came from both agonies—his to redeem the world from sin, yours to inspire generations until the resolution of that world's woes and throes.

As you sat in your Tower of London cell, praying with the accounts of Jesus' words and deeds in the garden of Gethsemane, you seem to have created for yourself a detailed examination of conscience. I picture you in the garden, pinching yourself to stay awake with Christ as he discourses privately with the Father. I see you keeping your eyes open at all costs, lest the Lord return to ask you, as he did Simon Peter, "Are you sleeping?" (Matt 26:45).

I cannot fathom the pressure you endured from your friends and family members, almost all of whom willingly made the oath, and many of whom, including your daughter Meg, pleaded with you to ignore the

---

8. Ratzinger, "Homily for Mass," para. 11.

impediment of your conscience. They did not consider the oath to be the end of Catholicism in England or a violation of divine law as you did, but the sheer weight of their supplications buckled the resistance of virtually all other men of consequence in England. I have personally viewed the petition which your king, Henry VIII, sent to the Pope requesting a divorce so that he could marry Anne Boleyn. His petition was put on display in the Capitoline Museums during my studies in Rome. Attached to the brown parchment with eloquent script are the red seals of the great men of your day. By affixing their seals to this request, they affirmed the king's right to the divorce, and later hailed him as head of the Church of England when he broke ranks with the Roman Pontiff. They were noblemen, members of Parliament, and bishops; you must have known most of them quite well. As I gazed upon that fateful piece of paper and the cracked seals, my mind turned to you and John Fisher, the only English bishop who refused to sign the oath and who, like yourself, laid down his life as a consequence.

Even at this most terrible occasion, you did not abandon your sense of humor. While providing for yourself an examination of conscience within your commentary on Jesus' agony, you gently chide your readers not only for sluggishness and sleepiness in prayer, but also for a lackadaisical approach to the sovereign Lord of the universe. I distinctly recall reading your list of mindless distractions which we indulge during prayer. When I scanned the lines containing your rant against picking one's nose while praying, I found my own finger scouring the inner sanctum of a nostril, more attuned to the discovery of the next booger than the meditation you were hoping I would focus on! I chuckled heartily, and I think of you now whenever the gold-digging urge threatens to overpower me in church.

The refrain of your meditations, so calmly and constantly asserted, is the need for vigilance—not necessarily against manifest evil, but rather the "sadness, fear, and weariness" which so easily creep into good hearts and swerve them from their holy purposes.[9] The metaphor of sleep, so personified in the drowsy apostles near Jesus as he sweats blood and offers himself to the Father, is both a reproach and a challenge to us who strive to fight as you did: nobly, calmly, with a steely resolve rooted in prayer. I think of your meditations, Saint Thomas, as a scriptural pep talk, a twofold encouragement coming from both Jesus and yourself, designed to sustain you then, and us now, when yielding or quitting seems much more desirable than perseverance.

9. More, *Sadness of Christ*, 17.

You were well aware that "other tyrants and tormentors"[10] would rise and dominate human affairs throughout the centuries. You were equally aware that the internal caesars of vice and sin are much more prevalent and even destructive of souls than external rulers. And yet regardless of the ruler, there can be no despair when the Lord of hope is invoked, and the light of fervent prayer in darkness surely generates confidence amidst great tribulation.

A quote embedded in my mind is the final petition of the entire book, summarizing everything in a humble sentence: "The things, good Lord, that I pray for, give me the grace to labor for. Amen."[11] Earlier in the meditation, you had noted, "We are reluctant to pray for anything (however useful) that we are reluctant to receive."[12] Your final request of the Lord, perhaps only days or weeks before you met the executioner's sword, is a reminder to us that boldness in prayer is itself a sign of trust in the loving Lord who bestows abundantly.

You knew, of course, how the story would end: the garden of Gethsemane prepares Jesus for Calvary, but that experience makes possible the glory of Easter Sunday. You foresaw the dissection of Christendom already underway in Germany and now in your beloved England, not to mention the forfeiture of your own head as an enemy of the newly minted head of the English Church. Yet there you were on the chopping block, at once forgiving your executioner and requesting that he not cut your beard, "For that," you noted, "has not committed treason!"[13] What a wonderfully strange quirk of final perseverance!

You were fond of saying to friends, "Pray for me as I will for you, that we may merrily meet in Heaven,"[14] especially as your entrance into Paradise drew near. I often conclude letters with that very same line, though I certainly hope to meet the addressee again here on earth before that final encounter. Since I never had the honor of dining with you at Chelsea, I will eagerly await a far more unforgettable banquet, full of mirth and puns and excessive displays of wit, assured that your prayers will help me arrive at the table without incident! And so I finish this missive with that same request: pray for me, good More, that we may merrily meet in heaven.

10. Ibid., 100.

11. Ibid., 155.

12. Ibid., 35.

13. Froude, *A History of England*, 276–77.

14. Rogers, *St. Thomas More*, 258.

Taylor Swift[1]

DEAR TAYLOR,

The monastery I call home has several young monks who are big fans of yours. Some won't admit to liking your music, but others heap unabashed praise on your albums, and most of us, if we were playing truth-or-dare, would confess to having celibate monk-crushes on you. After reading such a statement, you're probably thinking that you should cancel your Face-book, Instagram, and Twitter accounts, convinced that you cannot possibly achieve greater iconic status in your superstar social life.

My confreres and I lead a pretty different life from what you would consider normal. Our monastic life requires us to live in a community (think of a college dormitory, but with much more silence and an age range of twenty to ninety), wake up early, and pray at various points throughout the day. Unlike many monks, however, we also have a connection to the outside world through our mission of Catholic education. Teaching middle school, high school, and college students keeps us somewhat in tune with the "real world." It also gives us an excuse to stay in touch with cultural starlets like yourself, and to be aware of what our students are listening to and watching. If nothing else, it allows us to at least pretend to be hip when conversing with our students.

I can give you a few examples of this which, for better or worse, high-light your influence on my monastic and priestly life. There may or may not be a video of me belting out the lyrics of "Love Story" in a car with college students on the way to a campout. And there may or may not be photographic evidence of a monk clad in black and white taking the dance floor at a wedding reception, unable to restrain myself—excuse me, *him-self*—from busting a move when "Shake It Off" began to play. (Please note

---

1. Taylor Swift (b. 1989) is a very popular American singer-songwriter.

22

my preference for anonymity to protect my sources.) There may or may not even be a photo showing that I—I mean, that fellow—was involuntarily crowd-surfed during the song. If you wish to see these jaw-dropping realities, you should actually keep your Facebook active and send me a friend request, since I'm only on Facebook. Looking over this paragraph, I imagine Saint Benedict must be thinking there is no more hope for monasticism.

But back to you, Taylor. In my interactions with high school and college students, it is evident how many of them you have reached with your music. The word that keeps popping up with regard to you, especially among girls, is "relatable." The lyrics of your songs seem to come straight from your journal entries, because they have a fresh honesty to them that immediately resonates with your listeners. They relate to you in ways other music stars don't even want their fans to relate to them. I imagine many artists strive to create the soundtrack of a young generation, but your fans feel as though you yourself have gone through the same experiences that have happened to them, and that attracts them to you. Whether they are celebrating, crying, or just happily singing along to your tunes, you have a gift for providing music for the pivotal moments of young lives, and many people process their experiences and emotions by means of your songs.

I have also noticed, at least up until recently, how refreshing your choice of themes can be. No one else writes, credibly at least, about how much they love their mom, or muses on the pains of growing up and leaving childhood behind, or praises friendship as a worthwhile human institution, or dreams about breaking up a jilted lover's wedding. (Regarding that last item: for all your sweetness, you have always channeled a rather terrifying vengeance, and I am frankly relieved that I will never be an ex-boyfriend of yours.) Although I do grow a bit weary of all your love and heartbreak stuff (I never was a teenage girl, after all), you present even those topics differently from other artists, largely because most mainstream music is little more than mindless innuendo, or background beats for a sleazy music video.

So I was grateful to you for the way you refused to accept and promote cheap forms of love. It seemed to me that you encouraged young boys to dream of courting a girl honorably, and inspired young girls to dream of a noble prince who will treat them like the worthy princesses they are. Even those earlier breakup songs remind everyone that a girl's heart is not to be toyed with or abused, and boys definitely need to have that message drilled into their dense heads constantly. It's a downright shame that you are in the minority of artists that do this. So I want to encourage you to keep writing those lyrics that no one else writes, though I fear this encouragement is coming a bit too late.

I desperately wanted you to avoid falling into the same trap laid for so many young female artists: accepting the social pressure to conform to the stock-type of the angry, hyper-sensual, and nauseatingly selfish star who makes raunchy music videos to satisfy the lusty masses and withers the roots of her original musical passion. Recently, however, you did just that: you essentially killed off the old Taylor. I want her back!

I worry, Taylor, that in the midst of penning angry and vengeful lyrics and making senseless music videos channeling unproductive and narcissistic rage, you fail to realize how undistinguished and conventional you are becoming, even as you think you are creating a trailblazing new sound. But fear not: I am here to offer some solid life-coach advice! I would humbly propose an amazing and novel subject for a song that would surely be a smash hit on the airwaves, and perhaps offer a soothing balm to your soul scarred by lost loves:

You, Taylor, should write a song about nuns.

You probably weren't expecting that. You might even suspect me of being a total loser who writes lame letters featuring impossibly stupid ideas, but I am quite earnest. Let me explain the genesis of this idea, as well as why I think it is brilliant and a good career move for you.

I recently spent ten days hanging out with a group of contemplative nuns in Wisconsin. They belong to the Cistercian Order, just as I do, so that means we wear the same black and white clothes (except I don't wear a veil as they do, and they probably wash their habits more often). I took great delight in crashing a women's convent, even if it's not much of a party as Hollywood defines the term. Aside from celebrating Mass and hearing confessions, I gave an occasional conference on various religious topics, and talked with whoever wanted to chat with me about their relationship with God.

I must say that my monastic life is a cakewalk compared to theirs: they have to be in church at 3:50AM! (I was lazy and didn't get up to join them for their earliest prayers in those wee hours!) They observe a pretty darn strict form of silence, never leave their monastery except for the occasional doctor's visit, and have little contact with the outside world, aside from the altar bread they make and send out to parishes and monasteries (like mine) to earn their income.

The heart of their prayer, as it is for all monks and nuns, is the chanting of the Psalms. Try as I might to strain my marvelous falsetto to its maximum cadence, I could not reach their soprano pitch, so instead I listened to their chanting. In the midst of their singing one day, my attention began to wander, as it often does during prayer. (I like to think of my brain as a gloriously disorganized circus.) My meandering mind led me to ponder what you, a singer of songs and melodies rather different than Gregorian chant, would have to say about these nuns and why they do what they do. If nothing else, I think they have a devotion to music similar to yours—a passion even, a response to something they have experienced, an answer to a call they have heard.

It's easy enough to understand the spark of love between a girl and a guy and to write romantic lyrics about it; poets have done that for centuries. But what could possibly prompt a young girl to abandon absolutely everything in the "real world," promise never to marry or have kids or a job or a bank account, and to promise instead that she will pray several hours a day, wear the same clothes (and no makeup) for the rest of her life, be obedient to a superior, *and* hardly ever leave the convent? Sounds nuts, doesn't it?!

The nuns themselves would tell you that love motivates them to do all that. Now there are obviously a huge number of ways the term "love" is used (and abused) to encapsulate different realities. Love, as the nuns understand the word, certainly has a different definition than the one you sing about . . . and yet I consider their passion to be just as crazy, all-consuming, and worthy of throwing away your life for as you do about romantic love (in your non-breakup songs, of course). When a woman enters a convent, she entrusts herself entirely to God. Love impels her to make that choice freely, and to allow herself to be drawn closer every day to Jesus Christ.

The purity of their love is what astounds me, Taylor. They have absolutely no worldly motivation to enter a cloistered convent, no desire for fame or glory. They live quietly, totally out of any spotlight that could shine on them. They have precious little in the way of creature comforts—they only eat ice cream a couple times a year, for crying out loud—and yet they shine with a brilliance that convinces me they are truly joyful as they learn how to live for Christ, their heart's true love. They understand that the love which compelled them to enter the convent is not a fleeting feeling, but rather a commitment which frees them to love without compromise and without turning away when the feeling of being in love fades away. Their chant, together with their personal prayer and work, is a daily love letter to God, and they write a new page of that love story every morning.

Perhaps the best way to unite the love expressed in the chanting of the nuns and your singing can be found in Scripture. I have in mind one particular book from the Old Testament called the Song of Songs. When you read through it, you rightly think it's a random collection of ancient love poetry describing the desire of a bride to unite with her groom, who seems to draw away in order to stir up an even greater desire in her heart. The sensual nature of romantic married love is beautifully emphasized in this book of Scripture, as is the intense feeling of being madly enamored with someone. I think this is the aspect of love you typically channel in your music.

So what would a book like this have to say to a bunch of nuns who vow never to marry? Well, there is another way to interpret the Song of Songs. From a spiritual perspective, many writers have understood the beloved girl of the Song to represent the individual soul (or the church), and the bridegroom to represent God, manifest in Jesus Christ. The nuns, in other words, read the Song of Songs and recognize in its inspired words their own desire for union with God, expressed in marital imagery. The love of a nun for her Lord is not the same as a wife's love for her husband because the union is a purely spiritual one, but it is no less beautiful in its intensity and in the commitment it requires: "Set me as a seal upon your heart, as a seal upon your arm; for love is strong as death, and ardor is fierce as the grave. Its flames are flames of fire, a raging flame" (Song 8:6). For the nuns, that love for Christ can indeed rage, and should be fanned into a great flame, but they also know that their love demands a lifelong commitment which will require immense sacrifices, the most obvious being the lack of a husband, children, and career.

But they do not write breakup songs to God, Taylor. They undoubt- edly experience anger, confusion, and uncertainty about their relationship with the Lord, but grace allows them to trust in the love that initially incited them to abandon everything to follow Christ. God is always faithful to these nuns. He does not cheat them, or fail them in their time of need. Consoled by this knowledge, and painfully aware of their own sins and follies, the nuns simply persevere, and they in turn encourage their fellow sisters to remain faithful to their vows. I can almost guarantee that they would not want to trade places with you. It's not that they despise the glamour and glitz that define your public persona (in fact, they probably pray that you not fall into the trap of thinking fame to be the ultimate goal of life); they just realize that they have found a beautiful way of expressing their love for God, and they are grateful to be part of a community created to support them in their vocation to become happy and holy. Such happiness, totally elusive and unimaginable to many people in the secular world, is part of the "hundredfold" which Jesus promised even in this life to those who gave up everything (see Mark 10:28–30).

So yeah, you should write a song about love from a nun's perspective. Don't worry, Taylor—I am not demanding that you drop your career immediately and join a convent . . . though there is precedent for it. A woman named Dolores Hart starred alongside Elvis Presley and other dashing actors before shocking Hollywood in the early 1960s by entering a Benedictine convent just as her career was taking off![2]

Think too how wondrously liberating it would be if you never wrote another nasty venom-spewing breakup revenge song! If you want collaborators willing to craft that song with you, I would humbly suggest that you pay a visit first to the nuns, and then to my monastery in Dallas—Brother Francis and I do a wicked good cover of "Mean"!

2. See Hart and DeNeut, *Ear of the Heart*. HBO also made a documentary about her entitled *God is the Bigger Elvis*.

Heraclitus[1]

Dear Heraclitus of Ephesus,

You probably don't remember me, but a philosophy professor introduced me to you at the beginning of my junior year of college. The occasion was a semester-long fiesta called Ancient Philosophy, and you, at least for me, were the life of the party. Your wonder at the beauty of the cosmos was invigorating after the enlightened beatdown I received the previous semester at the hands of Hume, Kant, and Hegel. Truth be told, all of the pre-Socratic philosophers, not just you, fascinated me. I remember the thrilling sensation of grasping what Thales meant when he said that everything was water, and the joy of realizing how Empedocles could be right in asserting that love and strife govern every part of the cosmos and human life. There is an enduring freshness to the philosophy practiced by you and your Greek-speaking comrades that I found much more attractive than the analytic nitpicking I endured in other courses. I must confess, though, that a hopelessly romantic notion of the initial stages of philosophy clouds my judgment.

I hesitate to inform you that your book of musings, *On Nature*, survives only in fragmentary form. It was somehow lost in the flowing river of time, and we possess mere scraps of words and sentences of all the pre-Socratics, yourself included. The only reason we have even a glimpse of your actual text is because other philosophers and theologians quoted your words in their books. Their preservation of certain passages has ensured that your name is passed down along with these fascinating fragments. I suppose you will appreciate the mystique that attaches to thinkers like yourself who have been consigned to live only in the lines of others.

1. Heraclitus (ca. 535–ca. 475 BC) was a pre-Socratic philosopher from Ephesus. Only fragments of his works exist. One of the guiding themes of his philosophy is that all realities come into existence in accordance with the *logos*.

Anyone claiming that everything is fire is bound to gain a captive audience amongst pyro-happy male youth. I was particularly intrigued by your notion that an overall harmony is achieved by means of the co-incidence or unity of opposites: night and day are, you argue, one and the same, as each gives way to the other. The idea itself of unity emerging from multiplicity is not unique to you. Many of your fellow pre-Socratics preached something similar, and even the distant philosophy of yin-yang in Taoism stresses the harmony of sun and moon, hot and cold, etc. Regarding all things as one brings a sense of wholeness to all of nature and human existence. Thus you could say, in the most famous line that has been transmitted to us, "No one steps into the same river twice."[2] We think the river is the same, and yet the water in that river is ever flowing, changing while always maintaining its identity.

You say the same thing about fire, noting that it changes as it burns, while always remaining the same fire. For you, fire is the fundamental element of our material world. Instead of thinking that the world was created, you maintain that it is an "ever-living fire" which expands and contracts as time moves forward. The burning sun is new every day, even though it always remains the same sun.[3]

In other fragments, you talk about fire possessing the ability to reason or think. After a certain amount of time spent scratching my head, I reached a moment of insight as a college lad. If I understood your teaching correctly (which is far from certain!), Heraclitus, fire is merely a sign or manifestation of the ultimate source of law, harmony, and unity in the universe, which you call the *logos*. For you, the *logos* is divine and objective; it causes all things to come into being, and every rational being has some share in this ultimate *logos*. That doesn't mean, however, that everyone lives according to it—you have some scathing lines in which you claim that a majority of people live according to their own selfish *logos*, and even while awake act as they do when asleep, having tumbled out of the real world into a fantasy universe all their own.[4] Those who are fully conscious, on the other hand, come to realize that there is but one cosmos common to us all, one reality in which we all participate.

---

2. See a different translation offered in Heraclitus, *Fragments*, 27: "The river where you set your foot just now is gone—those waters giving way to this, now this."

3. Ibid., 21.

4. Ibid., 2–5, 60–61.

It is about this *logos* that I want to talk to you. In the fragments attributed to you, the word is a cause, the reason behind all things, and the source of unity binding all opposites together. In reading your assertion that fire, the symbol of the *logos* in our world of experience, is wise and rational, the thought occurs to me: Have you ever pondered whether the *logos* knew you, or even loved you? Aware that you are by definition a lover of wisdom, namely, a philosopher, I thought you might be grateful to hear the speculations of a fellow Greek-speaking lover of the *logos* who lived a few centuries after you. He is usually called an evangelist, since he proclaimed good news, but I consider him a full-fledged member of the elite club of wisdom lovers.

His name is John, and he penned a most extraordinary book that, fortunately, is not fragmented. He devoted the very first lines of his book, called a gospel, to an exposition of the *logos* as he understood it (John 1:1–5):

> In the beginning was the *logos*, and the *logos* was with God, and the *logos* was God. He was in the beginning with God. All things came to be through him, and without him not one thing came to be. What came to be through him was life, and the life was the light of human beings. The light shines in darkness, and the darkness did not overcome it.

After reading the opening verses of the Gospel of John, do you hear the same echoes of your teaching on the *logos* that I do? His description has much in common with yours, Heraclitus. The *logos* for John is the cause of all things, and sustains all things in being. There is even a brief reflection on the opposites of light and darkness, though I don't think you had such a moral meaning in mind with your take on opposites.

John begins his gospel with a central concept of Greek philosophy surely known to his Hellenized readers. A few verses later, though, something altogether unique and startling appears without warning: "And the *logos* became flesh and pitched his tent among us, and we have seen his glory" (John 1:14).

I would love to see your facial expression when you read that verse for the first time. This simple and awesome sentence highlights *the* crucial difference between your *logos* and John's, a distinction that has vast consequences for our understanding of the *logos* and our own relationship to it. Whereas for you the *logos* is a law, a harmonizing force, or a cold cosmic mind, for John the *logos* is *a person*, one who enters into relationship with all human beings. You probably noted that something was going on with the references to "he" and "him" in the prologue of the gospel, but the line in verse 14 is unmistakable and shocking: John insists that this eternal *logos*, this most glorious and unifying truth of life, became a human being at a specific point in history. The name of that human being, the *logos* incarnate, is Jesus Christ, and all those who read the Gospel of John as a word (a written *logos*) sent from God are called Christians.

I must tell you that I am not the first person to see parallels between your teaching on the *logos* and that of John. About a century after the life of Jesus, a Christian by the name of Saint Justin Martyr dared to call you and several other philosophers Christians, even though he knew that you lived before the time of Christ. He believed your insights into the *logos* were true, and that human beings possess the ability to know that there is an ultimate law accessible to us through our minds. Because of this, Saint Justin regarded your philosophy as a sneak preview of the full *logos* revealed by Jesus during his ministry. You had only a partial intuition of the full mystery behind the *logos*, since you were philosophizing before the supreme revelation of the *logos* had arrived on the earth.[5] But by living in accordance with the *logos*, you nevertheless scattered "seeds of the *logos*" in the fertile soil of the human heart, so that when the fullness of time came (Gal 4:4), men and women might be able to perceive in Christ the perfection of the truth you saw from afar:

> Therefore, whatever things were rightly said among all people are the property of us Christians. For next to God, we worship and love the logos who is from the unbegotten and ineffable God, since also He became man for our sakes, that, becoming a partaker of our sufferings, He might also bring us healing. For all the writers were able to see realities darkly, through the presence in them of an implanted seed of logos.[6]

At this point, Heraclitus, I think you can see why I asked you a little earlier whether you believed the fire or the *logos* knew you. Even if you did not, you are a precious witness to the way the human mind is blessed with the ability to reach rarefied heights and pave a guiding path for future philosophers to follow. I like to think your pursuit of wisdom in your native city of Ephesus prepared your fellow Ephesians, living centuries later, to receive the Gospel preached by Christian evangelists. One apostle in

---

5. See Justin Martyr, *First and Second Apologies*, 55: "And they who lived with the logos are Christians, even though they have been thought atheists; as, among the Greeks, Socrates and Heraclitus."

6. Ibid., 84.

particular, Saint Paul, worked tirelessly to sink the roots of the gospel deep into the hearts of the men and women of your hometown. Perhaps his exhortation to unity in a letter to them borrows, even if only as a faint echo, the language you employed to describe the harmony of opposites:

> For [Jesus Christ] is our peace, who made both one and tore down the dividing wall of enmity, abolishing through his flesh the law of commandments and legal claims, in order that he might create in himself one new person in place of the two, making peace and reconciling both to God in one body through the cross, putting enmity to death by it. (Eph 2:14–16)

Saint Paul is referring here to the unity of various ethnic groups who have come to believe in Christ; they are no longer Jews and Gentiles, but Christians, united as one body, as he notes further on:

> . . . exerting yourselves to preserve the unity of the spirit in the bond of peace: one body and one Spirit, just as you were called in the one hope of your call; one Lord, one faith, one baptism, one God and Father of all, who is over all and through all and in all. (Eph 4:3–6)

Heraclitus, I owe you a great debt of gratitude for stamping my impressionable mind with an admiration for the *logos*. What I found in the Gospel according to John perfected your initial glimpse of the *logos*, but I was able to see the fruits of the Gospel more clearly by standing on your philosophical shoulders. I cannot think of a more harmonious line for you than a verse in which Paul seems to be quoting an early Christian hymn, one whose words could have been penned by you (except for the part about Christ): "For everything that becomes visible is light. Therefore, it says: 'Awake, you who sleep; rise from the dead, and Christ will shine upon you'" (Eph 5:14). I am firmly convinced that you possess firsthand knowledge of the Lord and *logos*, whose dark mystery you penetrated so deeply without divine light. I therefore look forward to conversing with you someday about these wonderful matters.

Martin Luther King Jr.[1]

To the Reverend Doctor Martin Luther King Jr.,

Just before sitting down to write this letter, I listened to your "I Have a Dream" speech, given in front of the Lincoln Memorial on August 28, 1963. I have heard several other sermons of yours, and I must make a confession, from one pastor to another: I am awed by the power of your words. You measure the force of each syllable with grace, punctuate each phrase with the fury of the prophets, and demand a response from your congregation worthy of the faith raging in your words. The carefully crafted images, the gradual crescendo of your captivating voice, the syllables you lengthen with a strong trill, the manner in which you *will* your audience to believe every drop of honeyed text as you blend the end of one sentence into the next with unforgettable linking refrains—I believe that the Spirit was upon you, inspiring those who came to you hoping for justice, but hesitating to believe that it was possible. I must also confess a more humorous jealousy of your ability to elicit exultant choruses of "Amen!" and "Yessir!" and "Go on!" from your congregations. Simply put, Catholic priests can't preach like Baptist ministers, and the Catholic faithful just don't contract the same Sunday morning fever that your choirs and churchgoers do!

Your dream of justice and equality for black Americans, and of a country capable of holding hands together and sitting at the table of brotherhood, galvanized millions into peaceful action. That action, coupled with its righteous request, pricked the nation's conscience. No one doubts your singular role in startling our beloved nation out of its racist slumber and

1. The Reverend Doctor Martin Luther King Jr. (1929–1968) was a Baptist minister who played an instrumental role in the Civil Rights movement. He led boycotts, organized marches, and delivered unforgettable speeches, always employing non-violent means to achieve greater equality for African-Americans. He was awarded the Nobel Peace Prize in 1964, and was assassinated in 1968.

gaining for blacks across our land the right to use the same drinking fountains, restaurants, and hotels as whites, to vote, and to attend college as anyone else in America. Your life, so filled with what once seemed impossible dreams, was stopped when an assassin's bullet woke you to the eternal now of God's reality. Your cause, however, moved on, and many spoke of the election of an African-American President in 2008 as the crowning achievement of your movement.

But I write to you now, Dr. King, at another pivotal, and even perilous, moment in the history of our great nation. If anyone dared presume that America had successfully purged itself of the leprosy of racism in the decades following your death, they would be sadly mistaken. In recent years, the deaths of several African-American men at the hands of white police officers across the country have reignited the wrath of the black community, and outraged all peaceful Americans. The immediate availability of video allows everyone to judge the reactions of the police officers for themselves, and charges of widespread prejudice in some police departments have led to the formation of demonstrations to protest these abuses.

During one such protest in my own city of Dallas, Dr. King, a vocal but peaceful march was stopped by a madman's bullets. The shooter, a black man incensed by the deaths of black men at the hands of police, targeted police officers who were protecting the Black Lives Matter protestors marching against the displays of police brutality. He killed five of them before he himself was cut down. The shock of these cold-blooded murders prompted an outpouring of sorrow and support for the Dallas Police Department. The police chief, Sergeant David Brown, was a stoic and resolute leader in the days following. He calmly challenged those who desire change to find constructive ways of doing so, and I pray that his words will have their desired effect.

In the aftermath of this tragedy, Dr. King, I turned to the words of your most famous speeches in the hope of finding the proper response to such horrific violence. While you would rightly sympathize with the anger generated by the injustices perpetrated by some police officers, you would categorically reject any recourse to bloody retaliation. Leaders like yourself are desperately needed now, men and women who are learned and patient, who walk on the high plain of dignity and discipline, and channel righteous rage toward constructive, not destructive, ends.

I believe that your *Letter from Birmingham City Jail* is essential reading by all people, regardless of color, if we hope to overcome this latest manifestation of racial hatred. What I admire most about this letter is how calmly you set forth your argument. They are words of peace, but written with a sword for a pen. You do not sugarcoat any of the injustices you experienced in the hope of placating "prudent" men who urged you to passivity, and you certainly attack the reluctance of white church leaders to associate themselves with your efforts. The Christian gospel, given to all nations, is by nature blind to color. But habit and hatred, however subtle, are hard to overcome, especially when racism is sanctioned by apparently religious sentiments. There are, I'm afraid, still white congregational leaders today much like the ones you lament in your letter, ministers who are "more cautious than courageous and have remained silent behind the anesthetizing security of stained-glass windows."[2]

That sentence reveals the bold eloquence of a preacher, but the letter as a whole reflects a profoundly learned mind reaching back to the great thinkers of the past for inspiration in the present. Allusions and precise quotations form the backbone of the letter, and the people you enlist for your argument are mighty indeed: Socrates, Gandhi, Saint Augustine, Saint Thomas Aquinas, Martin Buber, and T. S. Eliot among them. As I read your letter, I wondered whether any political or religious leader today would be capable of marshalling the support of classical authors in defense of a righteous cause, such as overcoming racism. Our preferred means of national dialogue today seems to be a rapid-fire chorus of visceral reactions punctuated by screams and bilious rants on social media. They are a far cry from the reasoned and thoroughly considered letter-writing and speech-making which made your protests so successful. I would hope that the leaders of groups such as Black Lives Matter would return to you constantly to drink at the fountain of your wisdom and foresight, and that all African-Americans, who understandably feel threatened when they see such brutal videos, would continue to be inspired by your peaceful ways of resistance.

Just days after the shootings in Dallas, I stood at the podium of my church to proclaim the gospel and deliver a homily. The reading assigned for that Sunday was the Parable of the Good Samaritan (Luke 10:25–37). I would like to share that homily with you, Dr. King, because you were the primary inspiration behind it. In fact, the first quarter of my homily is a shameless copy and paste of an unforgettable speech of yours, though I withheld your name until I finished reading the quote for dramatic effect! My goal was to encourage an examination of conscience in my hearers

2. King, *A Testament of Hope*, 299.

through the characters of the parable, and to get my congregation to ask themselves what they could do to heal the wounds caused by the recent violence. What it lacks in rousing eloquence, I hope it makes up for in honest appeal to a properly formed conscience.

July 10, 2016
Cistercian Abbey Church

"'We use our imagination a great deal to try to determine why the priest and the Levite didn't stop. At times we say they were busy going to a church meeting, an ecclesiastical gathering, and they had to [hurry along] so they wouldn't be late for their meeting. At other times we would speculate that there was a religious law that [a priest or a Levite] engaged in religious ceremonials was not to touch a human body twenty-four hours before the ceremony. And every now and then we begin to wonder whether maybe they were not going down to Jericho to organize a Jericho Road Improvement Association. That's a possibility. Maybe they felt it was better to deal with the problem from the causal root, rather than to get bogged down with an individual effect.

'But I'm going to tell you what my imagination tells me. It's possible that those men were *afraid*. You see, the Jericho road is a dangerous road . . . In the days of Jesus, it came to be known as the "Bloody Pass." And you know, it's possible that the priest and the Levite looked over that man on the ground and wondered if the robbers were still around. Or it's possible that they felt that the man on the ground was merely faking, and he was acting like he had been robbed and hurt in order to seize them over there, lure them there for quick and easy seizure. And so the first question that the priest asked, [and] the first question that the Levite asked, was, "If I stop to help this man, *what will happen to me?*"

'But then the Good Samaritan came by, and he reversed the question: "If I do not stop to help this man, what will happen to *him*?" . . . Jesus ended up saying *this* was the good man, this was the *great* man, because he had the capacity to project the "I" into the "Thou," and to be concerned about his brother.'[3]

"Those words I just read, dear friends in Christ, are not my own; they came from the mouth of another pastor: Martin Luther King Jr. He offered this meditation on the Good Samaritan parable near the end of his 'I've Been to the Mountaintop' speech in 1968, delivered just one day before his

3. Ibid., 284–85.

tragic death at the hands of a mad assassin. The Church's liturgical calendar invites us to ponder this unforgettable parable this weekend, and I felt compelled to share Dr. King's words with you today, just days removed from the murders of innocent police officers a few miles from here.

"We have referred to our police officers, those slain on Thursday and those still among us, as heroes, as Good Samaritans, and rightly so. But the gospel parable requires us to examine *why* they imitate the Samaritan who had mercy on the fallen man, and *how* they fulfill the command of our Lord, directed at all of us, to 'Go and do likewise.'

"Jesus intended to shock his first century listeners with this parable. The Samaritans were distant relatives of the Jews, and both groups *hated* each other with the irrational wrath reserved only for the closest of human bonds. Saint Luke gives us an example of this revulsion at the parable's end: the lawyer cannot even bring himself to say the word 'Samaritan' when he admits that only the man from that despised group was merciful to the lawyer's fellow Jew agonizing on the side of the road. A present-day portrayal of the parable might feature a Palestinian coming to the aid of an Israeli, or an illegal immigrant from Mexico caring for a certain presidential candidate.

"Luke does not provide us with the Samaritan's motive for doing what he did, nor does he record the reactions of others listening to Jesus speak this parable. But the love clearly animating his actions is reflected in the question Dr. King puts in the mind of the Samaritan: 'If I do not stop to help this man, what will happen to him?' This man did not see race when he tended the enemy of his people lying half-dead on the roadside. He did not hesitate to sacrifice his time, his food, his drink, and his money to restore a fellow human being to life. He overcame the *fear* that sent the priest and the Levite scurrying to the other side of the highway, and he conquered the *anger* that must have tempted his heart as he approached the victim, the odious enemy of his people.

"That same heroic charity animates the hearts of the vast majority of our police officers. In carrying out their work, they reveal their willingness to sacrifice their lives, a willingness shared by Jesus when he took on human flesh to heal our wounds. (Let us also keep in mind that Jesus is at once the Good Samaritan and the victim of the robbers in the parable: he vivifies us as the divine physician, and suffers in our place upon the cross.) Only an unselfish heart can make a sacrifice of this sort. In such a heart as that which belonged to Jesus, the Good Samaritan, and the slain officers, there is no room for fear or anger, because perfect love, as we read in the

First Letter of John, casts out all fear, and channels anger to constructive, not destructive, ends.

"Dear friends in Christ, we all too frequently take the role of the priest and Levite in the parable, worrying about what will happen to us. We are too afraid to inconvenience ourselves, too angry to reflect peacefully, too devoted to our ignorant prejudices to listen to anyone who formulates a different opinion. A dangerous blend of fear and anger, two terrible spiritual cancers, is dominating our public discourse at present. Propagating fear in our community is nothing more than cowardly crossing to the other side of the road. To foment anger in the form of smugly self-righteous rants on Facebook, or to wait for someone else to enact a constructive solution, is to avoid the wounded heap of humanity placed in our path when it is our duty to give a reason to hope and a worthy cause to live for.

"I would ask you, brothers and sisters, to meditate quietly on this parable in the coming days, and to ponder your own role in overcoming your prejudices and binding the wounds of your neighbors, whomever they might be. We must pray for 'a kind of dangerous unselfishness,' to quote Dr. King again, the selfless mercy to perceive in our scarred brothers and sisters of any race, of any social status, the face of Christ. Each of us must discern calmly what he or she can contribute to the building up of trust and the eradication of injustices in our community. May we pray for the courage to love our neighbors as Christ loves them. May we acquire the wisdom necessary to confront injustices. And may the peace of Christ, which alone breaks down the wall of enmity and unites what men have divided, animate our every deed and word. Amen."

Any pastoral counsel or eloquence-enhancing suggestions for my sermon-making would be much appreciated! But more importantly, Dr. King, please pray that all of us now living in our beloved United States may foreshadow the eternal banquet of heaven by rejoicing and sitting together at the table of brotherhood here on earth.

The Sinful Woman[1]

To the woman whose sins Jesus forgives in Luke 7,

I am amazed by the fact that one single action in a human being's life can resound through the centuries, especially when nothing else, not even his or her name, is known. Such is the case with you. I cannot, unfortunately, grant you the basic dignity of addressing you by your proper name. When Saint Mark the evangelist presents the scene in which you anoint Jesus' head with perfumed oil as though in preparation for burial, he records the following words of Jesus in reaction to your gesture: "Amen I say to you, wherever the gospel is proclaimed in all the world, what she has done will be told in remembrance of her" (Mark 14:9). Your action has been faithfully preserved in the Christian tradition, yet your name is not attached to the church's earliest memory of you, recorded in all four Gospels!

Some fascinating similarities and differences appear in the four accounts of your encounter with Jesus. The version committed to writing by Saint Luke was one of the featured passages of my doctoral dissertation. Frankly, I wouldn't want you to read it, filled as it is with boring, footnote-saturated pages and a scholarly dryness that threatens to suck the life out of the gospel narrative. I am most grateful for my dissertation work, however, because my reading and study of Luke's Gospel raised many intriguing questions in my mind about your identity and the purpose for which Luke incorporated your story into his account of Jesus' ministry. What I could not question or answer in my dissertation, I want to ask you personally. Hence this letter.

1. The sinful woman meets Jesus in the house of a Pharisee named Simon in Luke 7:36–50. She anoints Jesus' feet with ointment, wipes them with her tears, and dries them with her hair. After comparing her gestures with Simon's lack of hospitality, Jesus declares that her sins have been forgiven. She is never named in the account.

I don't know if you were even aware that the early Christians decided at a certain point to commit their memories of Jesus' deeds and words to writing. Four books called Gospels, each containing sayings and actions from the life of Jesus, were composed after an initial period of oral preaching. This preaching probably took place when believers would gather on "the Lord's day" to break bread, reflect on how the prophets and the Law were fulfilled by Jesus, and share their personal reminiscences of him. As I mentioned earlier, all four Gospel writers included the scene in which you abruptly enter someone's home during a meal, and perform an act of love for Jesus which was met with criticism from others attending the meal. I would like to share with you the presentation Luke made of your gesture (the passage is found in Luke 7:36–50). In the course of relating his words, I will pose my questions regarding that wonderful encounter, and offer tentative answers that I have pondered and formulated over the course of much prayer and study.

One of the Pharisees invited him [Jesus] to eat with him, and after entering into the house of the Pharisee, he reclined at table (v. 36).

Only when I devoted myself to a careful study of the Gospels did I realize that Luke is the only evangelist who portrays Jesus eating in the house of a Pharisee. He presents Jesus dining with individual Pharisees who invite him to their homes on three separate occasions. Even after writing a 400-page brick of a dissertation, I still have no idea why Luke places such a distinct emphasis on Jesus at a table with individuals from the Jewish group that objected so vociferously to his ministry! I also find it interesting that Luke, who is setting the stage in this opening verse of the passage, omits the name of the Pharisee host. He will reveal it later, but we don't know who this man is right away, nor do we have any sense of his motive for inviting Jesus into his home.

Now there was a woman in the city who was a sinner. Recognizing that he [Jesus] was reclining in the house of a Pharisee, she brought an alabaster flask of perfume; and while standing behind him at his feet weeping, she began to bathe his feet with her tears. Then she wiped them with her hair, kissed them, and anointed them with perfume (vv. 37–38).

You come on the scene here, and I have many, many, *many* questions to ask you about these verses. Most people conclude that in identifying you as "a sinner in the city," Luke is implying that you were a prostitute. Whatever the sinful occupation was, I am more intrigued by the next line, because I desperately want to know *how* you came to recognize that Jesus was in the Pharisee's house, and what that knowledge reveals about your relationship with Jesus. Had you met him before you saw him entering the house? You must have heard of him at the very least. Perhaps the town gossip had reached your ears about a man identified (self-identified, or identified by others?) as the "son of God," "son of man," "Lord," and a "prophet." Perhaps you had heard the preaching of John the Baptist, the forerunner of Jesus who prepared the way for his ministry. But merely hearing about a holy man rarely induces someone to procure expensive ointment, bust into someone else's house uninvited, and steal the show with such an unusual outpouring of hospitality.

I suspect that you encountered Jesus face-to-face at some point prior to that meal. Even though Luke does not describe any such meeting, it makes sense to me that you had already presented yourself to Jesus as a sinful woman, and that your gesture of washing, drying, kissing, and anointing his feet was performed *in response to* something he had already said to you. One of my confreres in the monastery, though, is convinced that you met Jesus for the first time in the Pharisee's house! Was this an act of gratitude, a super-abundant burst of thanksgiving, or perhaps a penitential act in reparation for the sins he had spotted on your soul? I love the Gospels for this very reason: they give the necessary details of so many encounters between Jesus and a variety of characters, but they leave the backstory to the reader. What the evangelists leave out of their narrative, I suppose, is the designated material for our prayer, because it allows us to encounter Christ in some parallel way, and to respond with our own acts of faith, as sinners like yourself did in his presence!

When the Pharisee who had invited him saw this, he said to himself, "If this man were a prophet, he would know who and what sort of woman is touching him, that she is a sinner" (v. 39).

If I were in the shoes of the Pharisee host, I would first ask myself how you managed to enter my house and interrupt the dinner, not what Jesus is thinking! But I am curious why this man extended an invitation to Jesus in the first place. Had he, perhaps like you, listened to Jesus preach and been drawn to the message? I'm inclined to think that he wanted to find out for himself just how faithful Jesus was to his Jewish roots. Perhaps he welcomed Jesus into his home to interrogate him in detail about his interpretation of the Jewish Law—and he certainly got a firsthand glimpse of how Jesus construes it thanks to your intrusion!

The Pharisee, conscious of the rules against associating with unclean persons such as yourself, doubts that Jesus is an authentic prophet; if he were a faithful observer of the Torah as interpreted by the Pharisees, he would never permit a notorious woman like yourself to touch him. This action of yours disqualified Jesus in the eyes of the Pharisee host. Luke, however, does not provide further insight into the man's mind. Instead, Jesus launches into a dialogue with him:

"Simon, I have something to say to you." "Tell me, teacher." "Two debtors were in debt to a certain creditor; one of them owed 500 denarii, the other fifty. Since they did not have the money to pay him back, he forgave the debts of both of them. Which of them will love him more?" "I suppose the one to whom the larger debt was forgiven." "You have judged correctly" (vv. 40–43).

You momentarily disappear from the scene. I imagine you still kneeling on the floor, kissing and washing Jesus' feet, as he offers a parable to his host, whose name, Simon, Jesus reveals to the reader for the first time. I think everyone would agree that Simon answers Jesus' question correctly: of course the person weighed down with the larger debt would love the forgiver more! In the context of this scene, though, does Jesus want us to cast you as the person with the greater debt, and Simon as the one with the lesser? If so, what would Simon's sin, or sins, be? In the following verses, Jesus clearly suggests that a lack of hospitality is among them:

Then turning to the woman, he said to Simon, "Do you see this woman? When I came into your house, you did not give me water for my feet, but she bathed my feet with her tears and dried them with her hair. You did not give me a kiss, but she, from the time I came in, has not ceased kissing my feet. You did not anoint my head with oil, but she anointed my feet with ointment" (vv. 44–46).

Jesus makes a radical contrast between your loving actions and Simon's. In contrast with your superabundant love, the paucity of the host's love manifested itself in a failure to offer his guest the basic amenities of hospitality. I am struck by the repeated emphasis on Jesus' feet. In Matthew and Mark's versions of this story, you poured the perfumed ointment on his head, implicitly acknowledging his kingly status. There could be a focus in Luke's presentation on your humility: rather than "crowning" Jesus, so to speak, or anointing his body for burial, you humble yourself to the level of a servant. In the process, you would have implicitly taken on the posture of a beggar pleading for mercy. Then again, perhaps Matthew and Mark recounted a different event altogether—we know very little about how the Gospels were written!

I would love to know whether you had a hint about the next words that Jesus speaks. He directs his words to Simon, perhaps pointing to you as he lavishes praise on you. He continues in the next verse with what I consider the most important and mysterious line of the entire passage:

And so I say to you, her many sins have been forgiven because [OR that's why] she has loved much. But the one to whom little is forgiven loves little" (v. 47).

This particular verse makes biblical scholars scratch their heads. There is a big debate regarding the proper translation of one single Greek word: Did Jesus say that your sins are forgiven *because* you loved much in washing his feet and anointing them, *or* did he say that your sins are forgiven *and therefore* you have shown much love? In the first case, Jesus would be asserting that your loving actions have caused him to forgive you. In the second case, however, your loving actions would be the consequence, or result, of the forgiveness Jesus had already bestowed upon you. This second proposal harmonizes perfectly with Jesus' parable about the debtors, because the forgiveness of the debt brings about the love from the debtor. This difficulty, though nitpicky and grammatical, is an important one, because it affects the way we understand your relationship to Jesus, and our relationship to grace in general. Protestants will object to the possibility that any human action can bring about grace or forgiveness due to the totally corrupt nature of the human being; Catholics, on the other hand, while acknowledging our absolute dependence upon grace, are willing to assert that your loving actions move Jesus to forgive you.

I have a hunch that Jesus didn't intend for us to try to figure out the cause-and-effect relationship between your love and his forgiveness. Jesus definitively states that your sins are, or already have been, forgiven, and in the last verse of this passage, he directly speaks of your faith which has saved you (v. 50). *When did you make your faith known to him?* This brings me back to my opinion that you had a previous encounter with him, about which the text is silent. Were you converted from your sinful way of life upon hearing him preach, and resolved to offer him a proof of your repentance and desire to lead a new life? You obviously trespassed and carried an alabaster jar of perfume into the Pharisee's house with a specific purpose in mind. Could it be that Jesus has both your love and his power to forgive in view even before you perform your gesture?

He said to her, "Your sins are forgiven." The others at table said to them-
selves, "Who is this who forgives even sinners?" But he said to the woman,
"Your faith has saved you; go in peace" (vv. 48–50).

After speaking about you for several verses, Jesus finally addresses you
directly. Luke does not record your reaction. Instead, he introduces other
guests at the end of this scene. The reader wasn't aware of their presence at
the Pharisee's table until now, when they murmur about Jesus. Their question may contain an element of incredulity, and perhaps even scorn—after
all, it is God alone who can forgive sins. But did you see in their eyes perhaps a faint glimmering of faith, as they observe Jesus' encounter with you
and ponder the weight of his merciful words?

Jesus doesn't answer their question; he simply dismisses you after he
acknowledges your faith. I wonder why Jesus didn't permit you to stay for
the meal itself. Truth be told, the fact that you didn't eat at table creates a
problem for my theory that Luke highlights Jesus' ministry as one of sharing a meal with everyone—tax collectors, sinners, and even Pharisees. At
the very least, you recognized where to find Jesus, and you encountered
him in the context of a meal. This teaches us an important lesson about the
nature of the Eucharist, which we receive at every Mass: we are to recognize
the presence of Jesus, as the disciples at Emmaus did, "in the breaking of
the bread" (Luke 24:31). Maybe Jesus dismissed you out of consideration
for Simon, whose plans had already been disrupted quite radically by your
actions.

Regarding what happens next to you and to Simon, Luke is silent. He
simply moves on to the next scene, and doesn't give us any indication of
where you and the Pharisee go from there. *So what did you do once you*
left the house? Did you follow Jesus for the remainder of his ministry? One
tradition is that you are actually Mary Magdalene, but I have my doubts
about that. Luke mentions her in the very next scene (8:1–3), and he does
not make any connection between the foot-washing and what follows. Did
you fully convert from your sinful life, telling everyone of your experience
with him? Did you even die for your faith in the prophet who forgave you?

One of the reasons I love this passage so much is that it ends with
something of a cliffhanger. We don't know what becomes of you, nor do we
know how Simon reacts to Jesus' declaration of forgiveness. Luke doesn't
give us any clue as to what Simon thinks at the end of the meal. Do you
have any insight into what happened to him? Did he resolutely dismiss the
possibility that Jesus was a prophet, even the Messiah, on the basis of this

fateful meal in his house? Did he ultimately come to faith in the one who claimed divine authority to forgive sins?

I think the cliffhanger nature of this and many of Luke's parables is meant to draw us into the ministry of Jesus through prayer. In a strange but beautiful way, we the readers take on your role as well as that of Simon the Pharisee, and we answer the question of what happens after the scene by our own encounters and relationship with Jesus. Saint Luke has presented you as a model of repentance and love, and he wrote these stories down for our sakes, in order that we might "go and do likewise" (Luke 10:37, concluding the Good Samaritan parable). The story, in other words, continues through us. It is our privilege to read ourselves into these gospel scenes, so to speak, and to respond as you did to the call of Jesus. For your beautiful contribution to the Gospel, and for the humble anonymity that contribution required of you, I thank you.

Captain James Harvey[1]

Dear Captain Harvey,

My mother has a fascination with her family tree (her children playfully call it an obsession). About a decade ago, she began to seek information about her genealogical roots. She quickly threw herself into the work with tremendous gusto, eagerly pursuing the names and dates of her ancestors and the locations of their graves. In the process, she became a detective of her own biological past, an investigative journalist scouring genealogical websites and acquiring the resources needed to conduct a successful search for evidence on both sides of the Atlantic Ocean. Through a remarkable amount of sleuth work, she has filled virtually all the branches of her family tree dating back several centuries.

You should see her desk in the basement of my childhood home. I should rather say that you can't see it at all, stacked as it is with papers, folders, and binders! She tells me she knows where everything is, which means it's not messy. That same excuse was not valid when I was ordered to clean my room as a young lad!

An additional folding table has been enlisted to support the ongoing work. She has amassed countless binders and boxes full of every imaginable document: birth certificates, baptismal certificates, marriage licenses, census lists, ship manifests, immigration records, detailed city and neighborhood maps, military reports and discharge papers, newspaper clippings, photographs, last testaments, obituaries, death certificates, cemetery records. She has traveled to cemeteries in Philadelphia and Schuylkill County, Pennsylvania, historical research centers and parishes in Philadelphia and Ireland, and even the National Archives in Washington, DC, all for

1. Captain James Harvey (1810–1887) immigrated to the United States from Ireland and settled in the Philadelphia area. He served in the Union Army during the Civil War, attaining the rank of Captain. He is the great-great-great-great-grandfather of the author.

the sake of a crumb of knowledge about her long-dead relatives: a middle name, a date of birth, a maiden name. Whenever I return home, she happily updates me on her latest discoveries: the branch she has finally succeeded in identifying, the location of a gravesite, the clue which allowed her to unravel a difficult knot.

She goes about her work with a relentless but joyful determination to uncover dormant mysteries and forgotten persons. My siblings and I have been well acquainted with that zeal all our lives; I would claim that the Irish in her is responsible both for her genealogical fascination and her temper, occasionally and memorably provoked by her darling (but mischievous) children. Her persistence and incredible success in digging to the roots of her family tree has inspired me to bestow upon her the honorary title of *Mom Omnipotens*!

In the midst of this great detective work, she met you, Captain Harvey, and she has a particular fondness for you. That is understandable, at least in part, thanks to the abundance of information she has found about your life. In this letter, I would like to share with you what for me is a biography from the past, but for you is the résumé of your life. Think of this presentation of mine as merely the scratched surface of my mother's loving labors in your regard.

Your mother's name was Sara; she was born in 1779. You were born in 1810 in Ireland, County Londonderry. You had two older brothers, William and John, and younger siblings, Daniel and Catherine. According to census records, you and your brother Daniel must have left Ireland by 1831, perhaps in search of work. Apparently you went to Argentina first, and then came to settle in the Philadelphia area by the end of 1837.

You married a woman named Catherine Quigley, an Irish girl born around 1814. You had three daughters with her, all born in Philadelphia and baptized at Saint Augustine's Catholic church. One of those daughters, Mary Therese Harvey, married James J. Moran; their son, Thomas J. Moran, married Ellen Kirk; their son, James A. Moran, married Mary A. Kenny; their youngest daughter, Bernadette Moran, married Edward J. Coyle; their eldest child, Bernadette Coyle, married Paul W. Esposito; I am their eldest child. That brief genealogical layout makes me your great-great-great-great grandson. Happy to meet you at long last!

Your wife Catherine died in December 1843, a few weeks after giving birth; the baby, also named Catherine, sadly passed away just a few months after her mother. You married again in 1846, and your second wife was named Anna Farren. My mom has mapped out this side of our family tree as well—more on that later.

Your occupation as listed in census reports was a "morocco dresser" of leather. I had no idea what that meant, but mother dearest told me that morocco leather is the rich red kind used to make book covers, shoes, and purses. You treated skins of this type of leather by tanning and softening them. You identified yourself as the "superintendent of manufacturing" at a leather shop in Philadelphia (157 Willow Street, to be exact) before it folded. Mom has yet to get the official story on why you closed the business, but is determined to find out!

You interrupted your work during the Civil War, enlisting in the Sixty-Ninth Pennsylvania Infantry, Company D. My mom loves to talk about how your regiment was composed largely of Irishmen from Philadelphia who had formed neighborhood militias to defend their families from anti-immigrant and anti-Catholic attacks. You had attained the rank of captain in your militia, and that rank was honored when you joined the Union army. The neighborhood militia form of self-defense was all too necessary to protect yourself and your fellow Irish Catholics. I had heard previously of the vicious assaults made on Catholics and their churches by the bigoted anti-immigrant party which called themselves the "Know-Nothings" in the 1840s. I was shocked to learn that one of the churches they torched in Philadelphia, Saint Augustine's, was your parish church, and that you likely helped save the nuns who were trapped inside from being burned alive.

My mother is also proud that yours was the only Union regiment permitted to carry a green Irish flag into battle. You were injured at the Battle of Fair Oaks, part of the Seven Days Battle, in June of 1862. On the fifth day of the battle, your brigade was marching from Fair Oaks Station to White Oak Swamp when you tripped over an obstruction in the road, falling to the ground and rolling down an embankment. A family tradition, passed down orally, says that horses may have stomped on you when you fell. The Army surgeon who examined you wrote the following:

> Captain Harvey is affected with chronic rheumatism which there is reason to believe resulted from exposure whilst in camp before Richmond; an acute attack, having first seized him just after the Battle of Fair Oaks . . . He now has the disease in his hips and lower extremities and suffers very much from nocturnal pains and consequent lack of rest. He is spare and feeble, says he has lost

about 20 pounds in weight . . . In my opinion his disability at the present time is total."[2]

Given the severity of your injuries and general poor health (you were, after all, fifty-two at the time), you could not take part in the battle of Antietam, and were formally discharged on October 12, 1862. Your Sixty-Ninth Pennsylvania Infantry mates played an instrumental role in halting Pickett's Charge at the Battle of Gettysburg on July 3, 1863. My mom told me of the thrill she experienced at the National Archives in DC when she read your pension record containing your firsthand account of your sufferings, as well as the official discharge papers featuring the signature of General George McClellan. She also commented on the elegance of your handwriting.

You returned to Philadelphia a broken man, but you continued to work as best you could. Beginning in December 1862, you received a disability pension from the government of five dollars per month, which was increased to a whopping twenty dollars in 1886! You moved with your wife Anna to Chester, Pennsylvania in 1879. On February 7, 1887, you passed away. Your wife filed for a widow's pension (twenty dollars monthly), and her request was granted in 1888.

Captain Harvey, to be remembered in such a unique way is, I think, a gift. I spoke of my mother's fondness for you; she usually refers to you simply as "the Captain," and she has shown me a photograph of you—looking all dapper in a dark suit, with your hair finely slicked and parted—which stands on her desk. Beyond the gift of remembrance, however, is the greater gift you have posthumously granted your living descendants. In the course of her research, my mom, descended from your first marriage to Catherine Quigley, began writing to a certain Joe Donnelly, who traces his roots back to your second marriage with Anna Farren! They happily exchanged notes for several years, sharing their findings and family stories with one another, as well as raising further historical and genealogical questions to be pursued. You were the origin of their unlikely friendship and, quite literally, the meeting place for their first face-to-face reunion.

In 2015, I had the great privilege of accompanying my mom and dad to Philadelphia. We thought of you as we stopped in Saint Augustine's

---

2. Author's note: My mother, Bernadette Esposito, obtained this medical report on Captain Harvey after requesting his military service and pension records at the National Archives in Washington, D.C. She could not locate any further bibliographical detail about the note, aside from the request form itself that she filled out, which asked for the person's name, rank, and military unit. I trust that the doctor who examined the Captain will not threaten to sue me for copyright infringement!

church, where your daughter Mary Therese, my great-great-great grand-mother, was baptized. We also paid a visit to the national shrine where Saint John Neumann, whom mother is convinced confirmed you and other family members, is buried. She inquired about further cemetery records there, but did not get the answers she wanted from the secretaries!

The highlight of our trip to Philadelphia, however, was our visit to Old Cathedral Cemetery on a bright Sunday morning. The branches of your family tree embraced when Joe Donnelly, his wife, and son, met my mom, dad, and myself at your gravesite, where both your wives, your mother, your brother Daniel, and several of your children are buried. Joe Donnelly and his son are members of the Sixty-Ninth Pennsylvania reenactment group. They, along with several other men, dressed and outfitted themselves with the clothing and rifles of your brigade, and honored you with a brief ceremony and salute. I concluded our visit to the Harvey family tomb by giving my priestly blessing over your mortal remains.

These genealogical roots connecting generations, Captain Harvey, have brought great nourishment to my mother. What captivates me personally about her discoveries is the fact, so fundamental that its wondrous nature can't be expressed in words, that your life made possible my own. Our familial ties ensure that your story, however unremarkable it may have been by worldly standards, is my story as well. You might even be able to detect something of your personality in me, or even a physical characteristic we both share! What arises from this knowledge of my own roots is a feeling of closeness, of solidarity, with someone whom my mom rescued from the anonymity of history's paper trail.

From the perspective of secular history, your life illustrates the harshness and hostilities of immigration during the Know-Nothing period of the mid-nineteenth century, and gives me a share in those Civil War battles that I had learned about but never felt connected to. But from the vantage point of family and faith, I am very grateful for the continuity of generations binding me to you. My mom often speaks of her work on behalf of our ancestors as a form of intercessory prayer. The thought is quite a beautiful one—perhaps she has located a family member who had been forgotten, even if unintentionally, by his or her posterity, and had no one to remember or pray for them, until she took an active interest in her roots and returned their name to them, allowing it to rise like incense once again to God in prayer.

The step from this timeless form of kinship anchored in prayer to the Catholic understanding of the communion of saints is not far at all; in fact, it is quite a wonderful analogy. The wall of death separates you, my progenitor in family and forerunner in the Catholic faith, from me at present, but the spiritual communion generated by prayer penetrates that thin membrane and draws us close. We can aid each other as the mysterious workings of grace unfold in those of us who dwell, for now, in the land of the living. So pray for me, good Captain, that we may rejoice to meet each other on that eternal day of a glorious family reunion!

Deep Blue[1]

Dear Deep Blue,

The game of chess never interested me as a child. I received a chess set and beginner's book from Santa Claus when I was ten or so, but I never played with it. When Santa made that delivery, my parents were thrilled, hoping that Saint Nick's gift would unleash my inner chess prodigy and save them boatloads of money come college time. Alas, they hoped in vain.

I can't pinpoint a precise reason for my lack of interest in chess. I was a sports fanatic, and eagerly played any game requiring a ball and bodily movement outdoors, but I also liked to put puzzles together. I recently formulated a new hypothesis: that my less-than-wizard-level mathematical mind did not want to be exercised outside the classroom. Whatever the explanation may be, chess was simply absent during my childhood years. (As an adult, I have learned the basic moves and played perhaps five games, all of them devastating losses. I did shock my monastic brother once, though, by stealthily swiping his queen with a long-distance diagonal assault by my bishop. As I gloated, he proceeded to checkmate within three moves.)

While chess was never a part of my life, it was the sole reason for your existence. I am presuming that you, *if there is a "you" to speak of,* do not know either the history behind your creation or your experiences during your short life span. Allow me, therefore, to fill you in. Your genesis, Deep Blue, is quite an intriguing story. You were basically brainstormed into being by computer scientists from IBM, who developed and perfected your processing powers over the course of the late 1980s to the early 1990s. You, a sophisticated piece of artificial intelligence, were generated for one

1. Deep Blue was a chess-playing computer designed by IBM. It defeated the great Gerry Kasparov in a famous series of chess matches in 1997, one year after being defeated by Kasparov.

purpose alone: to prove that a computer could challenge, outsmart, and defeat a human grandmaster chess player.

Your team of handlers prepared prototypes and fine-tuned your software for a series of matches against the renowned and intense champion Gerry Kasparov. He beat you fair and square in 1996, but your computational powers were upgraded for the rematch in 1997. After besting the mighty Russian over six matches, the world hailed you as the bane of human chess players everywhere. Kasparov was convinced that some human interference played a role in a seemingly random move during one of the matches, but the IBM folks dismantled you without accepting the rematch which Kasparov demanded.

The news of your triumph reached me, though my pimply teenaged self did not ponder the implications of the result for very long. You have popped into my mind with some frequency, though, first during my studies in college, and now as an adult. While I profess total ignorance of tech talk and the science behind AI, I am fascinated by the positions proposed and affirmed by philosophers who muse on such matters. Near the end of my university studies in philosophy, I took part in a seminar dedicated to the philosophy of mind. One prominent group of philosophers engaging in this discourse, known broadly as materialists, insists that any and all functions of the human mind are reducible to brain processes, that is to say, are entirely and merely products of the physical and neural connections of our grey matter. Such a position leads some of them to say that the soul, traditionally defined by Greek and then Christian philosophy as the animating principle, or form, of the human being, is nothing more than the brain, and that the human brain is essentially a very complex computer.

You, Deep Blue, jumped to mind (or rather, my synapses fired a nodal memory of you across the axon pathways that somehow produce conscious thoughts and the sense that I think them) when I wondered what I had in common with a computer. While the notion of equating the human brain with computational hardware might baffle some and anger others, I did not dismiss the possibility as absurd. You immediately had the upper hand in my mind, since I had to grant that you would crush me in a game of chess. Once I got that concession out of the way, I proceeded to compare my human brain with your intricate rack of nodes and chips and codes.

My thoroughly unscientific study yielded the following results. The human brain does indeed have much in common with a computer; it should, after all, since human genius generated the idea and designed the hardware in the first place! Both are capable of receiving, categorizing, and accessing sensory input. The brain reacts to external stimuli processed by the senses and learns from experience (when a young boy touches a hot stove, he'll remember not to do that in the future!), while the computer follows its coded calculations in response to input from a keyboard or some other means of relaying a desired outcome. Both the brain and a computer are capable of analyzing possible outcomes and realizing those outcomes, whether in the form of a human action or a mathematical equation. I am fascinated by the thought that I am completely oblivious to the untold number of calculations my brain is doing simply to keep me balanced when I walk, or to maintain a constantly beating heart. Equally fascinating is the realization that at bottom, the computer can only do two operations: the addition and multiplication of zeroes and ones!

I recognize the same basic components in both structures, Deep Blue, but in spite of those similarities, something just seemed off in the comparison. The fact that computers are designed by human beings suggests that their manufacturing may reflect in some real way the thought and computational processes of the human brain. You might say that the computer offers a glimpse of a fraction of the human imagination made possible by the brain. And I see nothing wrong with admitting that a computer such as yourself can master a specific program such as chess and whip even the most gifted human master at his own game. Fortunately, there is more to human life than the ability to move a rook effectively!

Yet I wasn't content to admit that those similarities led to the simple equation of the human brain and a computer. What I felt was missing in the comparison was, quite simply, my humanity. The programming which goes into a human brain, for one, is innate in the grey matter itself in a way that simply cannot be duplicated in silicon chips. The process of developing neural pathways and learning to coordinate responses to sensory stimuli is a years-long process for a human being. Already while gestating in its mother's womb, the child's body is growing and developing at an incredibly rapid and marvelous rate, and that process only intensifies after birth. You, Deep Blue, had no infancy; you were simply assembled and booted up. Even if someone objected and retorted that a computer's infancy is its software development, I would say that the designers of the software are persons, not a computer, and no computer can replicate itself or create new processors without direct human intervention.

But I want to move to a broader look at the very claim materialists make, not about the brain, but about their own humanity. By asserting that their brains are nothing more than the sum of their psychosomatic interactions, they radically undermine the uniqueness of their being with respect to all other creatures. That is the conscious intention of many of them, I'm sure; the reduction of the human being to the level of a highly technical machine eliminates any supernatural or transcendent claims associated with man and woman, whether by philosophy or a religious tradition.

This reduction of the human greatly bothers me, Deep Blue. As I already mentioned, I readily acknowledge the fascinating comparison between my brain and a computer. I have no hesitation in affirming that the human being is an animal and can be examined as such, with the caveat that the human being is a uniquely rational animal capable of self-control and reflection beyond mere instinct. What troubles me is the willingness of so many biologists, neurologists, philosophers, and even ordinary men and women to undermine the sheer marvel of the human brain by aligning it with purely material causes. If the human brain is simply a computer, and the materialists are correct in asserting that all thoughts and dreams and actions are merely the product of brain states and axon snaps, then the possessive pronoun "my" in "my humanity" necessarily becomes an illusion, or at least a purely psychic experience generated by the firing of synapses. And if that were true, the very possibility of free will, and thus human personality, would be illusory as well, a purely biological phenomenon which produces in us the sensation of controlling our thoughts and feelings as though they did not rule us, but which ultimately would be a false sensation. In a strange way, materialists draw the same conclusion as the Buddha that the self is an illusion, but they do so from the opposite angle: materialists deny the spiritual reality of the human person, while Buddhism denies the material reality. The bottom line is that neither understanding accounts for a transcendent or even real I and you.

But my humanity, Deep Blue, my ability to think, to choose, to love, cannot be wholly reducible to brain functions or animal instinct. The machinery of your mind was nothing more than computational equations and heavy hardware; the machinery of my mind is moved by the lever of freedom. The very fact that materialists need to explain how and why such an illusory sensation as freedom is generated by the mind is itself a conundrum which cannot be answered by purely material causes. I am someone who chooses, who knows, who loves, *and I know myself to be such.* I could go further and confess that this is all possible because I have been chosen, I am known, and I am loved into existence by Someone, but I won't pursue that theological point (though see 1 Cor 13:12; Gal 4:9). I would rather say, as Saint Gregory the Great did some fourteen centuries before the first computer was created, that the machine of the mind is the force of love [*machina quippe mentis est vis amoris*].[2]

One of my confreres has a materialist friend from college who defines love as "an evolutionary positive adaptation designed for procreation and keeping family units together." To me, that statement is both true and incredibly insufficient to describe the nature of love and its effects on human life. Shakespeare himself acknowledged that "the world must be peopled," and the psychological attraction of love between male and female makes reproduction possible.[3] Yet could a definition of love not also make provision for totally non-evolutionary positive adaptations such as painting, storytelling, the making of books, music, gourmet foods, sports, pilgrimages, and charity toward the poor? Could it not also include the biologically unnecessary responses of awe to a stunning sunset or wonder at a philosophical argument? The force of love, I suppose, would be most evident in those activities that make us most beautifully human: friendship, inspiration for the creation of music or art, the ability to appreciate the creative work of someone else, the desire to know. From a more theological point of view, I think the force of love spurs us to come to the aid of brothers and sisters in need, especially the homeless and the sick. By adopting such a logic to inspire our free choices, we implicitly reject a survival of the fittest mindset by helping those who cannot help themselves, and open ourselves to be genuine instruments of spiritual grace in the material world.

But to return to you, Deep Blue, your sheer existence points to a reality which transcends the evolutionary and the purely material. Your makers brought you into being, and proceeded to give you a name and speak of you with possessive pronouns—this betrays our human instinct to transcend and personalize something that does not have any relational capacities whatsoever!

I recognize my dependence on my cortex and hypothalamus and all the other physical stuff in my head for all bodily functions, thoughts, and systems. The brain is indeed the most complex supercomputer ever built—yet for all that, I am not a robot. I may never convince a materialist of this,

2. Gregory the Great, *Moralia in Iob*, VI.27.58, 328.

3. Shakespeare, *Much Ado about Nothing*, Act 2, Scene 3.

because proof for him requires a purely physical demonstration of my transcendent freedom and rationality. I can in fact offer no such demonstration, since in using my brain to produce sounds and coherent language, I am always presupposing the rationality of my thoughts and words!

These musings, Deep Blue, are not merely a matter of dry philosophizing. As human beings continue to dedicate their neural synapses to building ever more complicated instruments, we must have a corresponding admiration for our humanity, and marvel at how uniquely and wonderfully we are made by nature. If we do not, we very well could find ourselves at the mercy of our own technological handiwork, whether of robots or drones or other devices, as Hollywood often hypothesizes in end-of-the-world blockbuster scenarios.

Perhaps what troubles me most about the materialist position is not the absence of any transcendent reality, but rather the implicit exaltation of utility which spurs philosophers, scientists, and lab technicians to tamper with human psychology and physiology for purely experimental purposes. Since every technical term seems to come from Greek, I'll employ the cool and true term *misophysy* for this phenomenon. Misophysy literally means "hatred of nature," and examples such as the genetic engineering of a perfect superhuman and the quest to find a cure for death all reflect this disregard for the boundaries which nature has *blessed* us with. If we use the technology we have created only for utilitarian ends, we wind up becoming machinelike ourselves, and think of others only in terms of the benefits accruing to us. The consequences of this mindset are disastrous for everyone but those who wield the power to impose their will and adopt a frightening attitude of materialistic divinity, even if that authority undermines or comes to threaten their own human agency.

We human beings should know that we deserve better than to be self-defeated by machines of our own devising. The mindset that our bodies and brains are mere hardware ripe for experimentation leads quite quickly, if left unchecked by natural moral restraints, to the destruction of the human in us, even as we madly celebrate the trend. Against this position, Deep Blue, there must be a persuasive way to root out the hatred of the human underlying many materialist pursuits. If we don't discover it soon, we might find ourselves checkmated by our own technological handiwork, or too ignorant of our free will to reverse the course our wanton use of technology has imposed on us.

Dr. Seuss[1]

DEAR DR. SEUSS,

This letter will begin much like the oodles of fan mail which surely flooded your mailbox on a daily basis. My siblings and I were normal American kids, and that means we loved your books. I fondly recall reading *Green Eggs and Ham* to my younger sister and brother in our familiar reading position: my sister snuggling next to me on the bed, my back against the wall, and my brother in my lap sucking his right thumb while holding his blanket and stroking my earlobe with his left thumb and index finger, calmly enjoying my hug as I held the book aloft in front of him.

We loved the loony and zany characters you created for our amusement. Our young imaginations gleefully followed your zigs and zags as we met Horton, the Lorax, Thing 1, and Thing 2. Your exclamation points and exotic fantasy places channeled a playfulness which nurtured our fertile minds into thinking of all the thinks we could think! *The Cat in the Hat* was dear to our young hearts, as was *How the Grinch Stole Christmas!*, but my absolutely positively favoritest book of yours was *My Book about Me*. Why shouldn't a book dedicated entirely to my discovery of my own wonderfully marvelous self, in which I was just as much an author as you, be number one?! I don't know whether my parents still have the book, but I would love to see how I wrote at the age of five or so. I bet my penmanship has only worsened in the decades following my initial attempts at clear and giant scrawls on your vibrantly colored pages! I vividly remember the joy of jotting down my personalized answers to the questions you posed: tracing the contours of my foot, noting the number of freckles on my face and keyholes in my house, walking the number of steps to the first tree outside the door,

---

1. Theodore Geisel, better known as Dr. Seuss (1904–1991), was a beloved American author of books for children. Some of his best-known titles are *The Cat in the Hat*, *Green Eggs and Ham*, *How the Grinch Stole Christmas!*, and *Oh, the Places You'll Go!*

and pondering my favorite animal. Oh, it was such fun to make my own book with your help!

Rather than continue to muse on *My Book about Me*, though, I'm hoping you'll go willingly on a tour led by me through another book of yours, *Oh, the Places You'll Go!* Sales of this classic, the very last book you published before your death, rise sharply during the springtime commencement season. I myself received this book as a reward for surviving college. As a graduation gift, the book is essentially a long congratulation, with fantastic illustrations of weird creatures and wild situations visualizing the excitement of a new chapter in the recipient's life. The story features one young lad possessing the freedom to tread any path he so chooses: "You're on your own. And you know what you know. / And YOU are the guy who'll decide where to go."[2]

As you know quite well, we cherish the sunny cheeriness of your exhortations, typically and relentlessly positive in their "mind-maker-upper"[3] sense of self-determination. Givers of *Oh, the Places You'll Go!* as a present understandably want to recognize a boy or girl's achievement and encourage them to look optimistically toward the future. Life beyond the finish line of school, after all, can present itself as an individual interstate of liberating glory: no more parental stop signs or scholastic red lights! You offer to the graduate a guarantee of personal triumph when one does whatever one wants: "Wherever you fly, you'll be best of the best. / Wherever you go, you will top all the rest."[4] Who wouldn't want to embrace the soothing promise of *FAME!* just for being and becoming whatever we wish, simply because we are innately awesome?!

Here's the place where this letter ceases to be regular fan mail, Dr. Seuss: I think *Oh, the Places You'll Go!* is an insidious book, whether for four-year-olds or 4.0s.

Putting aside the quaint pictures and following the narrative thread of *Oh, the Places You'll Go!*, I noticed that the lone primary character never interacts with *anyone* except in competitive terms, and he does not once perceive the need to seek or receive help along his way. A primary refrain throughout the story is the assurance that the unaccompanied lad's own wit and pluck will be sufficient to "un-slump"[5] himself out of any rough

---

2. Seuss, *Oh, the Places You'll Go!*, 2.

3. Ibid., 21.

4. Ibid., 15.

5. Ibid., 19.

spot and make him victorious over whomever is not him. The clear counsel given to wee ones and graduates alike is that you don't need anyone to guide you as your life "starts happening,"[6] and that you can get through the "Bang-ups and Hang-ups" and "The Waiting Place"[7] *all by yourself.* In theological terms, Dr. Seuss, this is pure Pelagianism disguised as the feel-good euphoria generated by the self-worshiping self, a mindset which today is obligatory in American pop culture and which, by extension, is totally destroying community of any sort, most especially (and tragically) the family.

"Oh don't be such a gloomily existential and pessimistic Grinch," I can anticipate you retorting; "it's just a children's book! And besides, I, the good Doctor, do point out that you won't always succeed. 'Sometimes you won't,' indeed, and sometimes you'll be stuck in the terrible 'waiting place' limbo of falling into line and being just an anonymous face in the crowd! I give good and innocent advice! So chill out and let the children be positively and unconditionally optimistic!"

While I do acknowledge that you concede the likelihood of occasional adversity and even failure (success is *only* "98 ¾ percent guaranteed!"[8]), the problem is precisely that this is a children's book. The attitude promoted within its pages trains the young to think only of their majestic "I" even before they go on YOUTube and fabricate their own social selves on Facebook and tweet how wonderful they are to their followers and no one in particular. To graduates, it plants the seeds for absurdly self-absorbed concepts such as "me-ternity leave" (which, by the way, treats motherhood as a selfish lifestyle choice affording unfair vacation benefits. The defender of such an absurd position has clearly never changed a poopy diaper, or groggily rocked a wailing baby to sleep at three in the morning). A friend who recently graduated from college told me that her bosses at the insurance company spent the first two weeks telling the new employees that each of them was the best of the best, but that each of them also needed to stand out and be competitive to get the edge. She pondered the long-term damage done to her co-workers by being told that they are demi-gods in a corporate *Hunger Games.* All awesome people are equal, but evidently some awesome people can make themselves more equal and more awesome than others!

In addition, the absolute individualist mindset espoused in your book prevents the possibility of true charity from taking root and bearing fruit in

---

6. Ibid., 9.

7. Ibid., 17, 23.

8. Ibid., 42.

one's life, given that charity by nature requires a communion of persons to give and receive love. No one else matters in *Oh, the Places You'll Go!*, and that is a recipe not only for personal mediocrity, but for lonely (and, what's even worse, unperceived) misery.

In this respect, I would not lump *My Book about Me* together with *Oh, the Places You'll Go!*, for the simple reason that *My Book About Me* requires the child to encounter *other people* in order to complete the book. He or she, after all, needs to acquire the signature of the mailman, write down the names of friends, and get help from Mom or Dad in measuring his or her height! This book highlights in a healthy way, I think, the early fascination with our unique selves, and it stimulates the wonder at being human so often extinguished by the time we reach adulthood.

Yet I think that the roots of egomania and self-worship are present even in *My Book about Me*, and that those same roots penetrate the soil of the reader's soul much more deeply in the beloved graduation gift. If relentless affirmation of their own wonderfulness is the exclusive voice children hear, will they not consider absolute praise and acceptance of whatever they insist on doing and being to be their right? And if they do feel entitled to be the kings and queens of their own ego world, can they possibly be happy in a life requiring community when their definition of happiness is based purely on the pleasure they can wring out of others (who, in turn, treat them according to the same utilitarian logic)?

I do not like this, Sam-I-Am.

You, Dr. Seuss, are a product of your time, as we all are, and *Oh, the Places You'll Go!* immediately came to mind as I read and learned about an American clinical psychologist named Carl Rogers, whose ideas seeped into pop culture in the mid-twentieth century. Rather than assess the merits of his person-centered therapy itself, which undoubtedly can greatly benefit those in need of psychological assistance, I wish to point out what to me are severely negative effects of Rogers's insistence on "unconditional positive regard" toward all human beings. Suspending judgment and allowing a person to reveal themselves without preconceived prejudices is certainly a good thing. As a secular cultural dogma though, this regard implicitly identifies any talk of moral evil within the human being as inhibiting a person's "becoming a person."[9] It admits of categories only in terms of feelings and personal comfort or discomfort, but never in terms of a good or evil

9. For a basic overview of Rogers's approach to psychology and therapy, see Rogers, *On Becoming a Person*, 3–27, 107–24.

recognizable to all; indeed, the human being, according to this mindset, is simply good, without any qualification or semblance of lurking shadow.

No surprise, then, that it also identifies the "happening" of a person to be the natural development which should not be stifled by guilt, sin, or constricting religious doctrines. Freedom to become whatever a person discovers they are becoming, without any specific goal besides the one(s) set by the one doing the becoming, seems to be the highest good and goal of Rogers's therapy. How can *any* common good be declared and pursued if every individual is an absolute, or if, as one Supreme Court justice put it, "At the heart of liberty is the right to define one's own concept of existence, of meaning, of the universe, and of the mystery of human life"?[10]

Dr. Seuss, I see Rogers's unconditional positive regard underlying almost every page of *Oh, the Places You'll Go!* I know it's only a children's book, and that I am a disgruntled monk with a keen dislike for Carl Rogers. But I do see a danger in the manner this mindset is continuously injected into the minds of American boys and girls. As a means of educating them about themselves, it certainly (and rightly) highlights the goodness and amazing nature of their humanity. It utterly denies, however, the lurking menace within that very humanity: the temptation to do what is not good, and in so doing to exalt ourselves as deities. Should we not rather teach our children that they are actually "ginks with a stink"—meaning an undeniably inherent (and quirky) goodness with a capacity for evil which we deny at our own risk, and which must be restrained—instead of almighty nomads embarking on a quest for a destination they'll figure out along the way without needing a map or assistance from anyone or anything outside their own will? Of course, sin, guilt, and other people (sometimes) are distinctly unpleasant, but what are the consequences of pretending that they do not exist?

Instead of a charity-numbing ego-stroke, Dr. Seuss, I would encourage gift-giving family members and friends to offer their children and graduates examples of unselfish love and greatness. Let them have Frodo and Sam, the heroes of the epic *The Lord of the Rings*, who had a cause greater than themselves to fight for, and who overcame their doubts by carrying each other's burdens. For the high school and college graduates, let them meet Dante the pilgrim, who needs Virgil and Beatrice to save his soul. Above all, let them hear the commencement address Jesus gives to his

---

10. See Justice Anthony Kennedy's majority opinion in *Planned Parenthood of Southeastern PA v. Casey*, 505 US 833 (1992).

disciples as he sends them on their missionary way: "Go then, and make disciples of all nations, baptizing them in the name of the Father, and of the Son, and of the Holy Spirit, teaching them to carry out all that I have commanded you. And know that I am with you always, until the end of the age" (Matt 28:19-20).

Eve[1]

Dear Eve,

A friend suggested that I begin this letter to you with the word WHY followed by many anguished-looking question marks. It would capture, he insisted, the universal lament generated by your fateful and far-reaching transgression at the dawn of humanity. I will resist such a temptation for two reasons: first, because it is impolite, and second, because I would rather practice the rhetorical technique of *captatio benevolentiae*, that is, getting on your good side early so that you will receive favorably the contents of this letter.

I do want, however, to remove a sneaking suspicion you might have regarding this whole "WHY?????" business. Let me be clear: I personally do not blame you, and I harbor no angry grudge against you, for my/our sorrowful lot in life. Time heals most wounds, and plenty of it has elapsed between you and me to soften my rage at the cause of humanity's descent into a destructive selfishness from which it cannot escape on its own.

Eve, you have acquired a really bad rap over the centuries, and all sorts of folks unleash torrents of guilt-laden scorn when bitterly invoking your name. They decry, of course, the woe which the original sin introduced into the Lord God's good creation. But thankfully, you don't need to be the proto-angry feminist and claim that misogynistic theologians, preachers, and others dump all blame for human frailty, sin, and death onto the XX chromosomes. Justice obliges me to note that the first man, your husband, is equally *if not more guilty* than you with regard to the sad story of the serpent's sinful and successful seduction of you. It was the man, after all, who had been charged by the Lord God to *guard* the garden *and you* from any

---

1. In the book of Genesis, Eve is the first woman created by God and the husband of Adam.

and all trouble. According to Genesis 2:15–17, both this command, and the corresponding promise of punishing death should he violate the command, were given to him before you were even created!

Indeed, the story of your tragic fall as narrated in Genesis clearly reveals that your Adam was *standing idly next to you* when the serpent began his slimy speech. Worse still, he remained totally silent, stationary, and lame when the occasion called for the courageous action of a guardian. How do I know your man was by your side, just as sure as you came from his? Well, Genesis 3:6 explicitly says, "The woman gave some of the fruit to the man, who was with her, and he ate." More evidence, however, is available: the serpent addresses you in the second person *plural*, meaning that he is sowing his seeds of suspicion and sedition not only in your ears, but in those of another nearby. The English language uses "you" for both the singular and plural, so most people don't realize that the snake is speaking to you as a pair. The only way to resolve this linguistic difficulty is for all Americans to start speaking Texan, a distinct subdialect of English, and begin to say "all y'all" rather than "you" for a plural audience.

But Genesis does indeed focus attention on your particular role within the drama, perhaps because the first Adam was too much of a passive meathead to warrant any psychological profiling. (He was created good in his pristine state, though, so I shouldn't be too hard on the fellow!) Immediately after the narrator notes that you and your man "were naked, yet they were not ashamed" (2:25), the slithery serpent slides onto the narrative stage (3:1). Your fateful encounter with him begins with a distortion of the Lord's command not to eat of the trees of the garden. The serpent introduces doubt into your mind, and you respond by misquoting the Lord's instruction to the man. The Lord had given him freedom to eat from any of the trees *except* the tree of knowledge of good and evil. The command forbade the man to eat, and the punishment was certain death; it said nothing about touching the fruit, which is what you add to the injunction (see 2:16–17; 3:3). You might respond to me by saying that you were simply thickening your defenses against temptation—the prohibition against even touching the fruit is more restrictive than not eating. Nevertheless, I think that your loose rendering of the Lord God's words gives the reader of Genesis an early hint that things are not going according to the original plan.

The serpent guarantees that you certainly would not die if you were to eat the fruit of the tree in the middle of the garden: "God knows that on the day you eat it, your eyes will be opened, and you will be like gods, knowing good and evil" (3:5). The following verses detail your downfall. The allure of the fruit, and the prospect of attaining the knowledge and divine status which God had unjustly withheld from you (so the serpent insinuated), overwhelmed your conscience. The next tragic verses (3:6–7) contain a beautiful synthesis of the manner in which weak human beings, myself included, yield to sin:

> The woman saw that the tree was good for food and was pleasing to the eyes, and that the tree was desirable to make one wise. So she took some of its fruit and ate; she also gave it to her husband, who was with her, and he ate. Then the eyes of the two of them were opened, and they knew that they were naked; so they sewed together the leaves of fig trees and made for themselves loincloths.

The emphasis, Eve, is on the eyes. The snake spoke truly when he promised that your eyes would be opened—the same eyes that beheld the attractive fruit also saw a changed world once you ate the fruit. In the popular mind, the fruit you plucked was an apple, but the Hebrew word simply means "fruit" of any kind. When Saint Jerome translated Genesis into Latin, "apple" became the obvious fruit of choice, because in Latin the word for apple is the same as the word for evil: *malum!*

The pure goodness of your created bodies, yours and the man's, is lost in the sinful act of disobeying the Lord's precept against eating the fruit. Your desire to know as God knows reflected your suspicion, fueled by serpentine logic, that God was malevolently keeping some secret truth from you. You had already known good and evil, for the Lord had arranged the good creation for you, with a minimum of prohibitions. Yet you insisted on what today is called self-determination, of arrogating to yourself the power to choose what is good and bad, right and wrong, without heeding any higher will than your own. A female friend of mine recently lamented that you had been emotionally unchaste with the serpent, allowing yourself to be entertained and openly tempted by his insinuations. You sinned as an individual, but every sin is shared in some way, at least in its consequences. And so you welcomed the supposed guardian of the garden to partake in your eye-opening misery, and together you recognized that your original nakedness was corrupted by your newfound sight.

And yet, when God comes to punish you both, neither of you feels the need to share the sin. What ensues is a classic psychological masterpiece of drama that I like to call the blame game. When you hear the Lord God walking "in the breeze of the day," (Gen 3:8) you hide from his presence.

The Lord God calls out to your man, "Where are you?" (3:8; that is the first question posed to human beings in the Bible, and God continues to ask each of us that question!). Adam confesses his nakedness, and the Lord deduces that he has eaten from the forbidden tree. So how does Adam respond? Does he man up and acknowledge that he utterly failed in his duty to protect you and the garden from any and all intruders? Hardly—the first words out of his mouth are, "*The woman*, whom *you* put here with me—*she* gave me the fruit from the tree, and I ate it" (3:12). He immediately points to you as the guilty party, but he also throws the blame back on God for having dared to give him a suitable partner who would lead him into sin!!! When the Lord turns to you, the reader might expect you to be the magnanimous one and accept the consequences of your actions; instead, you play the game and blurt out, "*The serpent* beguiled me, so I ate" (3:13).

The punishments promptly follow: first for the serpent, then you, and finally the man. The serpent is cursed, and is forced to crawl on its belly and eat dirt. Enmity will forever exist between human beings and snakes (3:14–15; more on that shortly). To you, the Lord God decrees that you will experience pain in bearing children, and that some disorder will exist in your desire for your husband (3:16). Because the man listened to you, the Lord curses the ground, and consigns the man to sweaty and toilsome labor in bringing forth fruit from that ground. The worst punishment of all, however, is the return to the ground from which the man came: "For you are dust, and to dust you shall return" (3:19). After providing you and your man with clothing, the Lord God boots you from the garden of Eden, thus beginning the human sojourn with banishment.

Your story, Eve, is an immensely powerful one, especially for people today. I think of the presentation in Genesis not as a literal historic event (no one was there to record it!), but as Israel's symbolic story of the beginning: an expression of the universal truth about sin and, in particular, its effect on the man-woman relationship. For one thing, God is described as possessing human attributes, fashioning the first man as a potter forms a piece of clay (2:7) and walking in the garden (3:8). These anthropomorphic details allow us to gain insight into the intimacy God wishes us to grasp about his relationship to us; God does not, however, have hands or legs, then or now!

In addition to that observation about the literary and not literal nature of these chapters, Eve, I see my own weak will reflected in yours and the first man's. I think the two of you represent every sinful human being, made of dust and destined to die. Genesis itself seems to give us license to interpret your very self and your actions in this way. *Adam* is not a proper name at the outset of this story; the word simply means "man" or even "humanity," a common noun in Hebrew. Only *after* the expulsion from the garden does your *adam* properly become *Adam*! You yourself do not even receive a name until *after* your sin; before that, you are simply "the woman." The proper name bestowed upon you by your husband literally means "the living one," and symbolizes your role in the history of humanity: "The man called his wife *Chavah*, because she was the mother of all the *chay*" (3:20; you have to pronounce that *ch* from the guttural depths of your throat, as though you were clearing out phlegm!). You are not a historical person in the past tense, but are rather present in every human being regardless of time and place. Whatever you do and think and experience, in other words, is meant to reveal to us what we do and think and experience; created good, we contravene the laws of God by sinning, and we die.

Yet the story of your seduction is not found in the first chapter of Genesis. We have to remember what comes before the original sin: the primordial goodness of God's creativity, a beautiful goodness still perceptible and desirable today, in spite of the bending of our will toward selfish sinfulness. When God creates in Genesis 1, he majestically brings forth the cosmos out of chaos, speaking, separating, and *seeing* (there's that verb again!) that everything is good and set within its proper boundaries. The crown jewel of God's creation is you . . . and me: "Then God said, 'Let *us* make the human being in *our* image, according to *our* likeness . . . God created the human being in his image; in the image of God he created him; male and female he created them" (1:26–27).

Ah, the mystery behind those pronouns! The Israelite authors of Scripture, Eve, were radically opposed to polytheism of any sort, yet the very first chapter of the Bible contains a reference to some plurality in God! What is clearly emphasized in these boundlessly fascinating verses is that the pinnacle of God's creation, the human being, images God most perfectly in the communion of male and female. The beauty of this complementarity is again revealed in the second account of creation, Genesis 2. In this chapter, God creates the man, *adam*, before the animals, and realizes that the man is incomplete by himself, unable to be complemented by any other created being. Whereas everything in the first chapter was "very good" once God finished creating, God admits in 2:18, "It is *not good* for the man to be alone." That's when you come into being. You are described as the man's helper, a partner. And the man's reaction when he awakes to find you by (and from!) his side is a Hebrew heart-melter of a love song: "This one, finally, is bone of my bones and flesh of my flesh. She shall be called 'woman' [*ishah*], for out of her man [*ish*] she was taken" (2:23). The man, in other words, is so ecstatic that he bursts into poetry, whereas previously he had simply grunted out names for the animals!

You have completed him, and his ability to relate to you draws him out of himself, to such an extent that he is willing "to leave his father and mother and cling to his wife, and the two become one flesh" (2:24). That complementarity, the unique ability to be made for and complete one another, not simply sexually but in terms of full personal communion, is a glorious if mysterious reflection of our creation by a loving God. This exquisite scene of your creation, so prominently featured at the start of the Bible, presents to us the roots of marriage as understood by the Israelites and then by Christians.

The goodness and love of God are abundantly manifest in the created world; that same goodness and love are again on display in the very act of your punishment. In the same moment as the doling out of punishments, the Lord also foretells the ultimate release from that penalty. We read in Genesis 3:15 a future-tense promise made by the Lord to the serpent: "I will put enmity between you and the woman, between your offspring and hers; he will strike at your head, and you will strike at his heel." In the Christian tradition, Eve, this verse has been labeled the *Protoevangelium*, the first announcement of the Gospel message. It foresees the arrival of a human being, born of a woman, who will save *adam*, humanity, from that original sin committed by you and Adam. Already in the book of Revelation, your offspring is identified as Jesus. His mother is Mary, and the serpent seeking to destroy him is "the dragon, the ancient serpent, who is called the Devil and Satan" (Rev 12:9). Jesus, on the other hand, is "destined to rule all the nations" (Rev 12:5) and to redeem humanity, restoring it to a wonderful and undeserved relationship with the Lord. Elsewhere in the New Testament, Paul refers to Jesus as "the last Adam," the one who overcomes the sin of the first Adam (see 1 Cor 15; Rom 5).

Good news indeed, Eve! Reflecting on that first Gospel message hidden already in Genesis, Saint Irenaeus, living in the second century AD, spoke of Jesus' mother Mary as your "advocate," someone who undoes the consequences of your action.[2] Irenaeus has a beautiful image for this: he

2. See this text in Richardson, *Early Christian Fathers*, 389–91.

talks about how Mary's obedient "yes" when she agrees to be the mother of Jesus loosens the knot of disobedience which you had tied around every human being in that first sin. As a result, through the sacrificial death of Jesus, we are freed from the burden of death, and are no longer bound by the law of selfish and slavish sin to a mortal existence.

The upshot of this *Protoevangelium*, Eve, is that Mary is already hidden within you at the dawn of humanity. She is entirely like you at the beginning: pure, entirely devoted to God, and opposed to evil. She even remains in you, however hidden, after the corruption of sin. God provides a way of redemption for the pitiful situation humanity falls into on account of sin, as evidenced by the promise in Genesis 3:15. In fact, God prepares Mary for her unique task of being the new Ark of the Covenant, bearing within herself the presence of God in the person of Christ, the healer and redeemer of humankind (see Luke 1:35).

So if Mary is hidden within you, that means that she dwells in every woman in some way. The inner beauty which allows Mary to image God more perfectly than any other creature is not lost by your original sin afflicting all the generations of humanity, nor can it simply be equated with motherhood. Through her humble obedience and willingness to be the mother of God, Mary allows us to experience the original goodness which God willed for you at the beginning. Beyond that, her son's victory over death also invites us to a more exalted position as inheritors of Christ's kingdom, even "sharers in the divine nature" (2 Pet 1:4). And perhaps this means that women today can look upon Mary as the model of their own inner beauty which, though wounded by sin, is worthy of being redeemed through her son.

All human beings, Eve, have sufficient personal experience with the distorted, egocentric lusts and passions which so quickly came to dominate you and then your children. That part of your story is all too easy to understand. What I hope we can draw from your example, besides the acute awareness of our wounded nature, is that men and women might call forth from each other the goodness that fundamentally remains within them. Your sin does not prevent Mary from revealing the purity and full beauty of womanhood, and the sin of Adam can, if we allow it, be conquered by the triumphal and sacrificial love of Christ, the second Adam.

Roberto Clemente[1]

To ROBERTO CLEMENTE, THE greatest Pittsburgh Pirate ever to play the game,

Among the treasured memories of my childhood are the times when my father spoke of his admiration for you. He was born a few years before you started your major league career, and grew up, like many Pennsylvania boys, idolizing you. His hometown of Punxsutawney, about ninety minutes north of Pittsburgh, was sufficiently far away to limit his opportunities to watch you from the bleachers, but the distance made those rare occasions when his father took him to Forbes Field for a game all the more glorious in his young mind.

One of the great unifying bonds between fathers and sons is the shared passion for sports. Already as a toddler, my parents tell me, I would hit and hold and toss any ball I could get my grubby little hands on, so I was ripe for inheriting my father's love of sports, particularly baseball. One distinct highlight from my early youth was a brief road trip, or rather a baseball pilgrimage, with my dad, our next-door neighbor, and two of his daughters. Our three-day trek took us to the three stadium-shrines nearest my hometown of Omaha, Nebraska: Kansas City, St. Louis, and Chicago (to see the Cubs, not the White Sox). I was hopelessly hooked on sports from a young age, though my love for baseball was crushed in the ill-fated 1994 season. I was visiting my grandparents that summer, and I attended

1. Roberto Clemente (1934–1972) was a baseball player who spent his entire career with the Pittsburgh Pirates. He was born and raised in Puerto Rico, and experienced a great deal of racism throughout his playing career. After hearing of a deadly earthquake in Nicaragua, he organized a relief effort. He was on board a plane loaded with food and medical supplies when it crashed en route to Nicaragua, killing him. The Baseball Hall of Fame inducted him almost immediately after his death; he was the first Hispanic to be inducted.

the Pirates–Expos game on August 12, the very last game before the strike cancelled the rest of the season. I never quite recovered my appetite for the game after such an atrocious display of selfishness on the part of the players and owners.

But to return to you, Roberto, I loved hearing my dad talk about the way you played the game. He confidently boasted that no other right fielder in the history of baseball had a stronger arm than you, who routinely cut down runners foolish enough to think that they could stretch a double into a triple, or tag at third and beat your laser throw home. Such boasting is obligatory and natural for your hometown team, of course! He recalled your uncanny ability to hit pitches way out of the strike zone, even spanking opposite-field doubles when an intentional walk pitch came too close to your bat. He spoke glowingly of the grace with which you carried yourself on the field, your ability to stop almost immediately after dashing from home to first base, your arms and legs flailing like octopus tentacles every which way. He told my brother and me about the thrill of hearing the radio announcer describe the bedlam after Bill Mazeroski's dramatic homer in the bottom of the ninth inning in game seven made the Pirates World Series champions over the Yankees in 1960. As a college student in 1971, he celebrated your other World Series triumph over Baltimore, in which you terrorized the vaunted Orioles pitching staff and won MVP honors.

My dad collected baseball cards as a lad (a hobby my brother and I greatly enjoyed as well when we were growing up), and delighted to have one of yours bearing the name "Bob Clemente" on the front, a shortened version of your name which, I later learned, annoyed you a great deal. He later lamented that my grandma dumped his card collection into the garbage while cleaning out his room—many of those cards are surely worth a stack of pretty pennies today!

My father could never end his reminiscing about you without referencing the way you died. He recalled how you recorded career hit number 3,000 near the end of the 1972 regular season, a double off the left-center wall in Pittsburgh's new Three Rivers Stadium (the Pirates now play in a beautiful gem of a park, not the concrete circle that was Three Rivers!). Though some people close to you insist that you were convinced you would die young, you presumably did not think at the time that your career hit total would be fixed forever at 3,000.

The reverence with which my father recounted the details of your final act of heroism has always stuck with me. One of your biographers, in fact, spoke of the entirety of your life as a "beautiful fury."[2] Your frantic sprints on the base paths mirrored, I think, your acute sense of social injustice and fearlessness in taking action when you perceived an opportunity to correct an offense. In the eyes of my father and the entire sports world, your efforts to aid earthquake victims in Nicaragua by gathering and sending materials from your beloved Puerto Rico, your anger upon hearing that the medicine and food were being diverted by the corrupt military regime, your decision to make sure the supplies reached their proper destination by boarding a death-trap airplane doomed to crash on December 31, 1972, hallowed you.

I remember my dad telling me about the rescue party sent into the ocean to search for your body, which was never recovered. Your close friend, Pirates catcher Manny Sanguillen, volunteered as a rescue diver for multiple days, refusing to believe you were gone. He even skipped your funeral Mass to continue the futile search in the silent waters.

Like other athletes who died while still in the prime of their lives, if not their careers, your passing granted you immediate entrance into the realm of baseball legend (sadly, death is often the prerequisite to acquire such immortality by worldly standards). You were elected to the Baseball Hall of Fame mere weeks after the plane crash; you and Lou Gehrig are the only players to be admitted without completing the five-year waiting period after retirement. As the first Hispanic to be enshrined in Cooperstown, your legacy has allowed thousands of boys from Puerto Rico, the Dominican Republic, Cuba, Venezuela, and elsewhere to dream of succeeding in the big leagues.

You suffered mightily during your career to secure this dream for future generations of Hispanic ballplayers. Though I knew you were born and raised in Puerto Rico, only recently did I learn many details of your constant struggles in the segregated America of the 1950s and 1960s. You had to play the racism game with multiple strikes against you: not only was your skin black, but you were also a native Spanish speaker in a thoroughly white and English-speaking part of the United States. I read that reporters would quote your broken English phonetically in their newspaper columns, a sign of vicious disrespect which rightly infuriated you. To your horror I'm sure, I must sadly admit that racism is still a scourge of our American society today, both against blacks and against Hispanics coming to the United States seeking a stable and hopeful future. The overt displays of hatred against you, such as segregated restaurants and hotels, might have disappeared

2. Maraniss, *Clemente*, 4.

(thank goodness), but a disgusting nativism seems to be reemerging today with growing virulence. I am continually shocked that a nation of immigrants, supposedly in an enlightened land of opportunity for all, should so wrathfully demonize groups of people who have a different shade of skin color and speak a different language.

Athletes today live in a thoroughly different world than the one you graced several decades ago, but I wish they would look to you as a model for their interaction with society at large. The deification of athletes in American culture, while an egregious mistake, nevertheless affords athletes a unique social platform, on which they can marshal public sentiment for righteous causes. Their primary task, of course, is to play a game, and I respect those athletes who wish to retain some semblance of privacy without involving themselves in cultural issues. Yet seeing how so many stars are consumed with the hype surrounding them that they end up being consumed by that very hype, your example of selfless service could galvanize an otherwise dormant conscience into action. Rare, for example, is the celebrity athlete who serves his (adopted) country—but you did, as a US Marine Corps reservist, no less. Your death simply accentuates the *donation* of your life, poured out in countless tiny gestures of friendship and solidarity over many years. How true and inspiring is the statement you once claimed as the motto for your life: "If you have a chance to make life better for others, and fail to do so, you are wasting your time on this earth!"[3]

My hope, Roberto, is that "the beautiful fury" with which you batted, ran, threw, *and lived* would inspire a new generation of Americans who might otherwise succumb to the temptation of accepting mediocrity or defeat when faced with adversity. As you were keenly aware, we waste our time on this earth when we never go out of ourselves and courageously serve those in need of our aid. My father was proud to pass along his admiration for you as a baseball player, but he was equally grateful that your awesome athleticism was coupled with a great love for your fellow human beings. Just as he shared his reverence for you with me, so too I hope that many other fathers would point their sons to you as a model baseball player and man.

3. Ibid., 322.

Saint Barnabas[1]

Dear Saint Barnabas,

Each year on January 25, the Roman Catholic Church celebrates perhaps the greatest conversion in her long history: that of Saint Paul. His dramatic encounter with the risen Jesus on the road to Damascus is narrated on three separate occasions by Luke in his book entitled Acts of the Apostles (chapters 9, 22, and 26). The movement of Saul from zealous defender of the Jewish Law and the traditions of his fathers to equally fervent ambassador of Jesus the Christ bearing the name Paul marks a pivotal turn in the young church's life. Paul reveals in several of his letters that he received a special commission from God to announce that salvation, once offered to the Jews alone, has been extended to include all nations, "the Gentiles," as well.

While all Christians should rightly praise the providence that produced such a fearless apostle, they should also remember that Paul's sudden allegiance to the Christian sect he sought to destroy created a huge problem for understandably suspicious believers in Jesus. Paul's newfound vocation as a preacher of the Christian faith was not hailed as heaven-sent by most. The great missionary work of Paul would have been unthinkable were it not for one courageous disciple who rarely gets mentioned nowadays.

That man is you, Barnabas. Please do not consider me a flatterer if I dare to assert that you are the true hero of the church in her first years of existence after Christ. What I know of you comes almost exclusively from Luke, the author of Acts, whom you must have interacted with at some point during your apostolic work, because Paul mentions the two of you in his letter to the Colossians (4:10–14). You might not have known that

1. Saint Barnabas (dates unknown) was one of the most prominent Christian missionaries in the first-century church. According to Acts of the Apostles, he is responsible for welcoming the newly converted Saint Paul into the Jewish-Christian community.

Luke was compiling a narrative of the first formative years of the church which highlights how the Christian faith spread from Jerusalem to "the ends of the earth" (Acts 1:8) and culminates with Paul's arrival in Rome. He introduces you in Acts 4:36 as a native of the island of Cyprus and a member of the priestly tribe of Levi. What he doesn't mention is how you came to know Christ, or why you abandoned whatever life you had led up to that point in order to follow his followers in Jerusalem.

You seem to have undergone a defining name change just as Paul did, for Luke notes that the apostles set aside your real name, Joseph, in favor of Barnabas, meaning "son of encouragement" in Aramaic. You were evidently a wealthy man; you sold a field and brought the proceeds to the apostles, laying the money at their feet for them to distribute as they saw fit (Acts 4:37). Luke does not tell his readers whether you stayed in Jerusalem or fled after the outbreak of the initial persecution against Christians, unleashed by none other than Saul of Tarsus and like-minded men (8:1–3), though Luke depicts you in Jerusalem one chapter later.

When Saul hears the risen Jesus ask "Saul, Saul, why are you persecuting *me*?," his transformation from zealous Pharisee to Christian apostle begins. After recuperating in Damascus following his blinding vision, Saul returns to the holy city of Jerusalem, seeking to align himself with the disciples of Jesus there. These followers of the Lord are afraid of him, well aware that the man now preaching that Jesus is the Messiah of Israel had previously tried to annihilate them. They are instantly suspicious of his motives, surely worried that he might simply be posing as a Christian to trap them (9:26).

In this moment of great tension for the young Christian community, you calmly place Saul under your care, bring him to the chief apostles (including Peter), and defend the genuineness of his conversion (9:27). Again, Luke does not explain how you came to trust that Saul was a legitimate Christian, or what prompted you to defend him when no one else apparently wanted to deal with him. Did you have doubts about his sincerity? Were you somehow instantly inspired to recognize in him God's chosen instrument to bring the Gospel to the Gentiles? The silence of the Acts narrative regarding your inner experience prompted me to write to you, and I am hoping you will satisfy my curiosity by filling in the details about your part in this drama! You might not have understood that your support of Saul was a heroic move that had immense consequences for the worldwide spread of the Gospel, but that is exactly how it appears to me from the unfolding of the church's mission.

Saul certainly rewards your vouching for him, because he becomes a companion on your missionary circuit. The apostles, according to Acts 11:22, send you to Antioch for what turns out to be a very successful mission to a vibrant and growing community. You rejoice at the fervor of this group of believers, and Luke describes you in 11:24 as "a good man, full of the Holy Spirit and faith" as you encourage (befitting your name) the believers to fidelity. You, having gone to Tarsus, found Saul, and brought him back to Antioch, seem to be the prime protagonist of this preaching mission. Luke confirms this in identifying you as the foremost "prophet and teacher" in the city of Antioch, where believers were called "Christians" for the first time (11:30; 13:1).

While in Antioch, the Holy Spirit instructs the believers there to set aside you and Saul for what comes to be known as the first missionary journey of the apostle to the Gentiles (13:4—14:28). I can imagine why you wanted to make Cyprus the first stop on the itinerary! Interestingly, once Saul meets the Roman proconsul Sergius Paulus on the island, Luke starts referring to him as Paul. From your island homeland, you missionaries sail to Asia Minor. One scene in particular from this voyage makes me realize just how lofty your status was not only among the first Christians, but among the very Gentiles you were evangelizing.

When Paul heals a crippled man in the town of Lystra, the pagan crowd thinks that the Greek gods have incarnated themselves in you and Paul, and attempts to adore the two of you. The people hail Paul as Hermes, the messenger god, but acclaim you as Zeus, the head of the entire Greek pantheon of gods (14:8–20)! Such worship of human beings, however much of an ego-stroke it must have been, naturally horrified your anti-idolatry sensibilities, which had strong roots in your Jewish tradition. You somehow managed to escape Lystra without the fawning mob trailing after you in adoration.

Your mission to the Gentiles brought to a head a defining issue confronting the early church. Many Christians today have difficulty understanding the debate regarding circumcision, since circumcision and the Jewish Law are such foreign concepts to us now. The fact that we are not familiar with them is a testament to the success of the discernment that you, Paul, and others made about the newness of faith in Christ and its consequences for believers.

Acts 15 is a fateful chapter for you, Barnabas. At its outset, Luke quotes speeches by Peter and James at the council of apostles organized in Jerusalem to discuss the relationship between Christians of Jewish and Gentile origins. Luke notes that you and Paul also describe to the assembly "the signs and wonders God had worked among the Gentiles" (15:12) through you—but he doesn't give a transcript of your actual statements! Ultimately, those gathered together determine, with the guiding aid of the Holy Spirit, that Gentiles should not be required to observe the precepts of the Jewish Law.

Acts 15 concludes with a brief paragraph indicating the existence of a rift between you and Paul (15:36–41). As Luke presents it, Paul encourages you to join him on another missionary voyage to return to the communities you visited and strengthen them. You want to bring along John Mark, but Paul apparently refuses to accept him for this mission. This John Mark, after all, had abandoned you all on the first journey, jumping ship in 13:13, and Paul "insisted that they should not take along with them someone who had withdrawn from them in Pamphylia, and who had not accompanied them in their work" (15:38). You clearly take John Mark's side (according to Colossians 4:10, you and he were cousins), and your disagreement with Paul grows so sharp that a separation takes place: you and John Mark go to Cyprus, and Paul acquires a new traveling companion, Silas, and heads for Syria and Cilicia.

Although Acts continues for thirteen more chapters after your parting with Paul, Barnabas, you do not make another appearance in the book. In fact, Luke follows Paul on his various voyages, at times even writing in the first person plural rather than the usual third person singular. One possible explanation for verses such as "Having sailed from Troas, we headed straight for Samothrace" (16:11) is that Luke himself joined Paul at these points on the missionary itinerary, and wrote from his own travel diary of the experiences. At any rate, the second half of Acts is dedicated entirely to Paul, and finishes with him hanging out in Rome, having brought the Gospel from Jerusalem to the capital of the world empire.

Barnabas, what startles me about the way Acts ends is that you, an indispensable leader of the early church, faded into total obscurity at the expense of Paul, the man whose evangelical career you made possible. Frankly, that doesn't seem fair, though I should immediately add that the fault does not lie with Paul for this state of affairs. In a handful of Paul's own letters, we get a fortunate glimpse of a reconciliation between Paul and John Mark (Col 4:10; 2 Tim 4:11; Phlm 24). Paul also mentions you in 1 Corinthians 9:6, meaning that you must have been known to the Corinthian community in Greece even though Acts does not state that you set foot there. Many biblical scholars suggest that Paul is referring to you when he speaks of "our traveling companion," the "brother praised for his preaching of the Gospel among all the churches," though Paul keeps him anonymous (2 Cor 8:18–19).

The first years of the fledgling church, Barnabas, are a source of endless wonder for me. Although the seeds of my Christian faith were obviously planted by Jesus himself, they were first cultivated by men such as yourself, who carried the fledgling plants and set their roots in the soil of so many different nations. Sadly, it seems as though you went from being the main man in the early Christian community to a relatively unknown figure, destined to stand in the shadow of Paul whenever church history is documented. Did you have any inkling of this? Were you aware that Paul was writing letters to the communities he founded that would one day comprise half the New Testament, the second part of the Bible?

As I wrote at the outset of this letter, I believe that you are a singular hero in the life of the church, and I simply wanted to thank you for your humble witness. Our lack of attention to your life can, I think, be instructive for Christians today: it can remind us that we must be content with the role God gives us to play in the drama of salvation. We may be asked to strut in the spotlight for a time, and then labor silently behind the stage curtain, as you did for the rest of your days. (By the way, did you die a martyr? The church's tradition says yes, but we lack definitive proof.) I like to think that you happily accept a quiet profile at this point in the Christian story. After all, your contribution is noted in the early chapters of Acts, and the part of your mission known to us, faithfully carried out, was of crucial importance in charting the course of the Christian faith. In the end, I imagine that you are perfectly content to yield the historical limelight to Paul, since you have better things to ponder now than fleeting earthly fame. Seeing you celebrate your victory of faith with Paul is a joy I hope I am privileged to experience someday, with the help of your prayers.

Kisa Gotami[1]

Dear Kisa Gotami,

Some individuals have such an impact on history that the names of others associated with them also resound in stories and songs. From a religious perspective, the radiance of a single influential leader may be reflected by a disciple. In that way, the teachings of the master are often communicated through an eyewitness who experienced their dynamic presence or received their teaching firsthand. Such is the case with you, Gotami. Thanks to a record of your interaction with the Buddha, I acquired a profound insight into your master's teaching on the nature of suffering and death, and I am eager to share my reflection on that insight with you.

The following is a summary of the account I received of your meeting with the Buddha.[2] I present it here in the hope that you would correct whatever part of it I have misunderstood. The story goes that you were a poor woman, disrespected by all on account of your poverty-stricken upbringing. You managed to gain a measure of respect after marrying and then bearing a son, who became the light of your life. Your son, however, died unexpectedly at the age of four or five. Immense maternal anguish seized you, and your neighbors thought you had gone mad when you carried your dead son in your arms and wailed from door to door, "Give me medicine for my son!"

While everyone else mocked you, a wise man understood that sorrowful agony had compelled you to such a desperate and pitiable measure. He instructed you to visit the only person who would be able to prescribe the proper remedy for your condition. And so you walked to a nearby monastery and sat in the congregation of the Buddha, known as the

1. Kisa Gotami (ca. sixth century BC) was a woman living in India who became a disciple of the Buddha.

2. Burtt, *Teachings of the Compassionate Buddha*, 43–46.

Tathagata—the one who has transcended suffering and passed beyond all temporal phenomena and desires.

After you shouted your desperate request for medicine, the Buddha saw that you were ripe for his teaching. Rather than provide a healing herb or an ointment for your son, he told you to go through the city once more and collect grains of mustard seed from every house in which no one had ever died. You were initially thrilled to receive this command, thinking perhaps that the Buddha would use these seeds to restore the life-breath to your son's inanimate body. But you were not able to gather any mustard seeds at all. For whenever you made your request, your neighbors sighed and confessed that death had struck many in their homes. An illuminating insight soon came to you: the *Tathagata* must have wanted you to realize that no one could collect any seeds, given that death has touched every house without exception!

This awareness then prompted you to walk outside the city to "the burning-ground," which I presume is equivalent to a cemetery. Upon that ground, you placed the lifeless body of your son, and there you left it. On returning to the Buddha, you reported that you had successfully grasped his teaching, and had no mustard seeds to show him. You then entered upon the path of discipleship, leading to the enlightenment that the Buddha wishes all sentient beings to attain.

As I understand your story, Gotami, you successfully relinquished your emotional hold on your son, recognizing that you could not resuscitate him. But you also overcame your instinctive desire to retain him somehow, discerning in that attachment a desperate clinging which would only generate further inconsolable anguish for you. The Buddha's teaching enlightened you chiefly because it taught you that the way to eliminate suffering is to eliminate its cause—namely, the aching sorrow that led you to bewail the loss of your child.

Your story, Kisa Gotami, was my first introduction to the teachings of the Buddha, and my further readings in Buddhism, though hardly exhaustive, have not produced a more eloquent or succinct presentation of its principal aim. I was immediately captivated by the sense of serenity which I perceived in your relinquishing. The teaching that life is fundamentally *dukkha*, suffering, resonates with those who comprehend that everything under the sun is fleeting and destined to fade. But instead of an all-consuming grief, or a bitter resignation to such a pained and profitless fate, you acquired a most noble peace, a cooling of the inferno that *is* human desire, and which produces such seemingly limitless pain at the loss of a loved one.

Indeed, the four noble truths enunciated by the Buddha offer a most attractive path to someone like me, long inclined to the tranquil acceptance of all things taught by the Stoics. To learn that life is fundamentally suffering, that the cause of suffering is desire, that to overcome suffering one must overcome desire, and that to eliminate suffering one must follow the Noble Eightfold Path—all of this had an alluring and calming effect on myself, who had so often been ensnared by the fetters of desire. I know that once Siddhartha Gautama found enlightenment and became the Buddha, he dedicated himself to spreading the good word of his insights. He became an itinerant preacher aiming to alleviate the suffering of being trapped in the illusory world of desire. The one good desire, as I understand the message of Buddhism, is that of wishing to liberate other beings from ignorance, shining the illuminating light on their path in the hope that they too might eliminate their own desires and, by definition, suffering, thus attaining the cool extinction of all reality, *nirvana*.

The Buddha's motive in teaching all sufferers his noble truths was *karuna*, an overflowing compassion which seeks nothing more than to break the bonds which chain beings to the world of the senses, a false and fleeting domain of selfishness and suffering. In my own tradition, I found a striking parallel to the figure of the *bodhisattva*, a person who has nearly attained the cessation of all desire, yet vows to bear the burdens of untold numbers of sentient beings and remain in the illusory world until that suffering has ceased. In the Jewish and Christian traditions, the Suffering Servant of Isaiah 53 comes immediately to mind. This servant is an innocent sufferer whose wounds heal all those enmeshed in sin, and give life to all who had been destined for death. For Jews, that figure seems to represent the nation of Israel itself; for Christians, it is Jesus Christ.

What I mean to say in all of this, Gotami, is that I owe the Buddha a profound debt of gratitude, but not in the manner you might expect. I am grateful to the *Tathagata* not because I converted to Buddhism (I did not), but because he made me a better Catholic priest. That might seem paradoxical, but hopefully I can explain what I mean.

When I became a priest, I immediately recognized how essential compassion had to be in my ministry. This need was most manifest when I heard the confessions of men and women whose sins were weighing them down and preventing them from walking on the path of joy and grace.

They came to me seeking to alleviate their guilt, and to overcome their sins. They desired nothing more than to experience the mercy of God channeled through my forgiving counsel and absolution. Even today, I am constantly awestruck by the nature of my priestly privilege. I am blessed to look upon these people with compassion, with a love drained of any egoism, and desiring only to help them emerge from the swamp of sin in which they have mired themselves. Though my primary teacher in this regard was most certainly Jesus, the Buddha's sermons had an immensely consoling effect on me. I hope to communicate the same healing compassion which you experienced when you came to him in your hour of need. You experienced liberation from the plight of suffering, and penitents receive the grace-generated freedom of their release from sin in the sacrament of confession.

Your master's teaching has also borne fruit in my role as a spiritual director. Many men and women cling so tenaciously to already-committed sins and grudges and failures and regrets that they gradually regard them as indispensable to their life, as a tragic comfort they cannot do without. The Buddha would speak of this, and of the general suffering which defines existence, as an arrow lodged in a person's chest. The origin of such an irrational effort to keep the arrow in their chest, of course, is a dominating desire that refuses to let go of any number of emotions or experiences—anger, lust, and envy are chief among them. These are spiritual cancers, and if allowed to grow, they will eat away at the soul and happiness of the person who allows them to survive. If I can succeed in pointing out the peace that comes from cooling those disordered passions, if I can counsel people to release their iron grip on what they know they need to part with, and if I can get them to relinquish their desire to hold onto past events and grievances which make them miserable in the present, then I will have helped them dislodge the arrow of desire piercing their spiritual chests.

Yet I fully grasp that my experiences in confession and spiritual direction cannot merely be the fruit of the *Tathagata's* counsel. For just as I became a more compassionate priest through the Buddha's good words, I also noted the vast abyss between the ultimate goals of the Buddhist and the Christian life. For the Buddha and you, Gotami, the noble truths assert that the elimination of suffering requires the elimination of desire *and that the elimination of desire requires the elimination of the self, of the sense that I am someone who thinks, feels, and hurts.* That self-identity must be extinguished, much like a burning candle-flame snuffed out by a pair of fingers. The idea of personhood seems to be at the source of all desire, and thus is the problem to be overcome. The very roots of the Christian understanding of the human person and God, however, presuppose the goodness and reality not only of the created world, but of personhood itself. The height of the Christian mystery, I believe, is my personal encounter with others and, ultimately, *the* Other, an exchange of love which requires and generates communion.

I am still amazed at how close to Christianity the Buddhist solution to suffering is, and yet at the same time how infinitely different in aim. While the emphasis on compassion unites these two traditions, I can't help but regard the elimination of desire depicted in your story to be terribly cold, and almost *inhuman*. My intention in confession and spiritual direction is not to bring men and women to initiate the cessation of their humanity, but rather to be *more fully human*. And by that I mean that I want them to perceive how they are loved by God and are capable of returning that love to him through the love they show to others and to themselves.

From my Christian perspective, Gotami, the need to purge myself of impure and disordered desires resonates perfectly with your master's teaching on the suffering those desires produce. Yet I cannot stop desiring any more than I can stop thinking, for I regard my "I" as a gift, and myself as a being made for real communion with others. That desire for communion, ultimately with God, prompts me not to annihilate my desires (and, eventually, my very self), but to purify and channel them to their proper end. If I can look upon my fellow human beings with compassionate and priestly eyes, I can ease their burden by carrying it as far as I am able. The ultimate result of my life's work at this compassionate purification of desires, mine and those of others, will be (I hope) a beautiful glory which eye has not yet seen. It will not be, I believe, the melting of myself into nothingness, but rather a vision, face-to-face, of the One whom I was made to see and love.

But I have not had this experience yet, and while I sojourn here, as a human and as a priest, I hope to continue my purification. I would ask you, Gotami, to correct whatever deficiencies you detect in my understanding of your master's instruction, for I would not dare claim to understand it fully, or to have summarized it worthily. I wish to end by simply thanking you and the Buddha for the part you played in helping me learn to be more compassionate.

Nike[1]

To NIKE, THE GODDESS of victory,

The Louvre Museum in Paris showcases a most exquisite statue of you as the centerpiece of a grand many-columned hall. The marble sculpture was unearthed in 1863 on the island of Samothrace, where your cult was especially strong in ancient times. Though lacking a head and arms, the piece depicts you striding confidently forward, the light garments draped about your female form billowing back as you majestically slice through the air. According to Greek mythology, you flew around battlefields and athletic contests, announcing the name of the victors and richly rewarding them with glory and fame guaranteed to outlast their mortal bodies. The most stunning aspect of this sculpture is the pair of wings attached to your shoulder blades. The artist, an unknown genius with hammer and chisel, carved such delicate yet thick feathers as to make a modern think that he photographed a falcon's wings and reproduced them in marble on your back.

As the victory goddess, your favor was desperately desired by warriors, athletes, poets, and political leaders alike. Your fame did not cease with the end of the classical Greek age and the death of the gods. Victory, the glorious triumph over an opponent and personified in your allegorical self, is still actively pursued today by the same groups of people. In fact, I would dare say that you are still worshiped—no longer in a human form, but by means of your name and a logo, both of which are adored by more men and women than your Hellenistic sculptor could possibly have imagined.

You will be flattered, I suppose, to know that you were the inspiration behind the creation of a line of shoes and clothing (even though athletes

---

1. Nike is the ancient Greek goddess of victory. She is the namesake of the American shoe and clothing empire whose symbol is the "Swoosh."

competed barefoot and totally nude at the original Olympic games). Aptly called Nike, the company rapidly catapulted to the pinnacle of success not simply in athletic merchandise, but in American culture as a whole, to such an extent that it forms minds and dictates fashion styles by its advertising and the omnipresence of its logo. The word "Nike" no longer needs to be featured in ads, since the "Swoosh" is perhaps the most recognizable corporate symbol in the world (though probably second to the golden arches, that ultimate signal of culinary decadence). Sponsored athletes pitch the products, thus generating the must-have mentality in kids and adults who idolize their sports heroes. The Swoosh is plastered on shirts, jerseys, shorts, socks, soccer balls, baseball bats, sweatbands, water bottles . . . and shoes.

I only made the connection between you, the Greek goddess, and the shoe company as an adult, standing with mouth agape before your statue in the Louvre. In retrospect, I realize that my initial adoration of you came long before that aesthetic experience. I must confess that I was already paying homage to the shrine of your Swoosh as a fifth grader. Hoops season was about to begin, and my growing feet needed to be fitted properly with basketball shoes. My father drove me to the nearby sporting goods store, presumably calculating what he was willing to pay for a decent pair of sneakers. He was not committed to any particular brand, and he always insisted that the quality be high *and* that the price be reasonable for our athletic purchases.

I, however, walked into the store knowing exactly what I wanted. Earlier in the week, I had seen TV and magazine advertisements for Nike's latest dunkalicious product: the Air Zoom Flight, worn by All-Star point guard Jason Kidd. Those ads never reveal the price of the shoes, of course, and money was the last worry in my ten-year-old brain that day. I was consumed with unbridled lust for the Zooms, because they would ensure that I would be the talk of the fifth-grade classroom *and* that I would dominate on the court by channeling Jason Kidd's mad ball-handling skillz.

I dreamed about those shoes before going to the store with my dad. As soon as I spotted them on the shoe rack, I resolutely refused to look at any other pair from any other brand. I oozed with awe at the awesomeness contained in the sleekest footwear I had ever beheld. The black and white checkerboard pattern on the carbon fiber pods bulged out from the sides, giving the impression that they were full of air to send my vertical leap skyward. Luscious and smooth white foam surrounded the alien-eyeball pods lining the entire shoe. The obligatory black Swoosh was embroidered, bordered by silver thread, on the right side of the toe. Sick and slick black suede comprised the top of the masterpiece, which also came equipped with a black mesh tongue, black-and-white shoelaces, and a killer tag on the back of the shoe that spelled "Flight." Ah, I remember my rapture well. Those kicks looked like astronauts on the moon would wear them, and *I wanted them*—no, *I craved them*—certain that they were designed to launch my hoop dreams into intergalactic All-Star celebrity orbit.

The trouble was, they cost $110, and my allowance didn't exactly provide me with the funds I needed to cover what dad was unwilling to pay for. So I did what any kid does when their reasonable parents object to forking over an excessive amount of cash for a trivial good: I went petulant, and refused to leave the store until dad caved to my craven desire for the Zooms. I think he ultimately relented not only because I was relentless, but because dinnertime was approaching and he was hungry. Our car ride home was passed in edgy silence, my poor dad angrily staring at the road and wringing the steering wheel with tense hands, I clutching the orange Nike box close to my heart, unwilling to be separated from my precious jewels.

I hadn't even walked into Mrs. Paladino's classroom the next day when my basketball teammate Mark saw me strutting down the hallway and exclaimed, "OHMYGOSH—ESPO [that was my nickname] GOT THE ZOOMS!!!" I was the most popular kid in the class that morning, and my materialistic triumph felt *good*. Even when the fawning attention of my fellow students was distracted by recess, I maintained a feeling of invincibility (as your name, which means "victory" in Greek, suggests). The certainty that my glorious self was incapable of anything but swishes and pinpoint assists and glorious victory as long as the Zooms graced my feet kept me floating with great expectations.

Until I wore them to basketball practice, that is. I quickly grasped, to my horror, that my coveted moon boots, purchased at great cost to my father's wallet and emotional tranquility, rubbed my pinky toes raw, and I couldn't slide properly in them. Their wavy soles prevented my fleet feet from getting good traction on the court, and within days, I was forced to find a new pair of basketball shoes just to keep my toes in fair condition. Naturally, the Zooms were too scuffed up to be returned to the store for an exchange, and I think I asked my mom to take me for the second purchase to spare my dad any further sole (or soul!) anguish on my account.

The lesson this young lad learned, Nike, although I am still slow to implement it fully, is that unrestrained lust for stuff generates only a constant unease and an insatiable grasping after petty objects. Now, I do not blame you for this abject example of wasted idolatry from my youth. Much like the other gods and goddesses of Greek myth, you are a projection of particular emotions and ideals common to all human beings, then as now. If we can speak of a multitude of primordial sins *always* plaguing the human heart, greed, and the innate feverish obsession to be first and famous and fairest, are certainly top-tier ones. An unreflective devotion to you was manifest in my mania to possess the newest, shiniest, most popular item on the market. The Nike empire had successfully convinced ten-year-old me that the crowning achievement of my life was to be a walking billboard for their logo and their motto, "Just do it"—which, by the way, might inspire athletes to excellence, but subliminally tempts shoppers to yield to their purchasing impulses.

My story has all the frivolity and hilarity of youth associated with it, but the dominating allure of all things Nike only dawned on me when I removed myself from the market-driven world. That step out of the daily force-feeding of images and ads and slogans has allowed me to realize the power of victory when put to materialistic purposes. It has also alerted me to the blatant absurdity of living solely to possess items that will wear out, fall out of style, get lost, and pass into oblivion in a matter of months.

Allowing faithful servants of the Swoosh to think of themselves as "valued customers" at best and at worst as slaves to what fashionistas they have never met deem worthy of stylish devotion, seems a pitiful reward for the money poured into a logo (and one imported from morally dubious labor facilities in China at that). After so many pairs of shoes, untold shirts, shorts, and socks purchased in order to be sacrificed to you, after the mountains of cash spent in the hope of luring your heart to bestow triumph, after the unperceived brainwashing of a mad culture obsessed with image and incapable of delivering happiness, after all that loyalty, I ask: What has the Swoosh done for *me*? Where are my Zooms now? Why do I no longer feel the urge to bow down before you, fair goddess, and seek your fickle patronage? I'll provide the answer: we are logo-obsessed beings, Nike, but I realized (eventually) that only the *Logos* was worthy of my worship. May others come to the same realization before they blindly sacrifice to the Swoosh in the vain pursuit of what material goods can never provide: victory over their own weakness and temptations.

Jonathan[1]

Dear Jonathan, son of Saul, the King of Israel,

Human nature has not changed in the three millennia separating your life from mine. The surest proof of this statement lies in literature. The earliest epics and sagas written in all parts of the earth reveal the same dreams, desires, and tragedies pulsating through the human heart and expressed in action and interaction with others. The passions of love, greed, envy, joy, and sorrow are vividly portrayed, from *Gilgamesh* and the Hebrew Bible down to *The Lord of the Rings*, an epic written in recent years. But while the desires animating the human being are fundamentally the same, their expression can change, and their definitions can even shift. I would like to share with you a relatively recent interpretation of love and relationships which directly involves you.

All that I know of your life comes from the Bible, specifically the books of 1–2 Samuel. I presume that these works were not familiar to you, since they recount, among other things, your death and several decades of history afterward. Though I trust that these books present an account of your life grounded in factual history, I cannot obtain any certainty on this score, nor can I confidently distinguish historical fact from the literary contributions of the author. I will therefore give a brief summary of the presentation the inspired writer or writers of these books recorded concerning you.

They tell us that you were a son of Saul, the first king in Israel's history. After young David saved the army of Israel by defeating Goliath the mighty Philistine, your father became violently jealous of the victorious lad, and basically went mad obsessing over how he might eliminate David, whom he feared would seek the throne which was rightly yours to inherit. In multiple

---

1. Jonathan is a biblical figure found in the Old Testament books of 1–2 Samuel. The son of Saul, he was a beloved friend of David, helping David when Saul grew jealous of him and attempted to murder him.

verses, you are said to have loved David as your very self (1 Sam 18:1, 3; 20:17). You protested David's innocence to your father, and withdrew from his presence to inform your friend of the king's plot to kill him (1 Sam 19:1–7; 20:1–42). You handed over to David your own cloak and tunic, as well as your sword, bow, and belt (1 Sam 18:4). David managed to escape Saul's murderous reach, which prompted the king to curse you for aiding the enemy and to slander his own wife, your mother, for bearing such a son (1 Sam 20:30). At a designated spot in a field away from the king's house, David the outlaw bowed down to you, the prince, three times, and you kissed and wept together before parting (1 Sam 20:41–42). The two of you met again when David was on the run, and you concluded an astonishing covenant, in which you voluntarily renounced your own birthright and claim to the throne by asserting to David, "You shall be king of Israel, and I shall be second to you" (1 Sam 23:16–18). You and your father Saul died in a disastrous battle against the Philistines (1 Sam 31). When David received word of your deaths, he chanted a mourning song of praise for both of you. Of you, he sang, "I grieve for you, Jonathan my brother! You have been most dear to me; more wonderful was your love to me than love of women" (2 Sam 1:26).

David "loved" a riotous number of women according to Scripture, so that last statement is rather striking. It has, in fact, been the primary piece of evidence for an interpretation of your relationship with David which has become increasingly popular in the last century or so. Proponents of this interpretation assert that your relationship with David was a gay romance. Based on the biblical texts alone, Jonathan, I don't think that position can be refuted. Old Testament passages are often spare in the details we value in our modern literature, such as the internal thoughts or feelings of a character. While 1–2 Samuel do offer some insight into your mind and David's, enough lies unsaid between the lines to admit the possibility of a romantic relationship between the two of you.

While I recognize the possibility of the position put forward by those who favor a homosexual interpretation of your friendship, I do not think the author of 1–2 Samuel intended this conclusion to be drawn. One specific reason comes from the long tradition of Scripture interpretation which draws out the meaning of a particular passage in light of other passages. Given the resolute prohibition against homosexual actions in the Torah (a prohibition which extends into the New Testament and the Christian moral tradition), I find it highly unlikely that you and David would be praised without reserve in other biblical books if your relationship was in fact erotic.

We read several times that you loved David "as your very self" (1 Sam 18:1, 3; 20:17). To my mind, this repeated statement suggests that we should consider you a model of the commandment "You shall love your neighbor as yourself" (Lev 19:18). Jesus quotes this verse as the second part of the "greatest commandment," the first being to love the Lord with all your heart, soul, mind, and strength (Mark 12:28–34, based on Deut 6:5). Given what Jesus incorporates into the greatest commandment, I would argue that 1–2 Samuel portray your interaction with David as a profound example of male *friendship* (*philia* in Greek), and not an erotic homosexual relationship (*eros*). I hope you don't mind if I explain why I think this way.

The interpretation which romanticizes the love between you and David seems to ignore, or at least minimize, an essential component of *friendship*, which guided you to risk your life for David. What I mean is that you revealed a love not to be equated with lust or even emotional self-interest, but a selfless giving and cooperating with the will of God on behalf of David and, ultimately, all of Israel. True *philadelphia*, literally "brotherly love," certainly allows for affection to be shown. You beautifully demonstrated this by selflessly sacrificing your possessions, prestige, and even your life.

Unfortunately, Jonathan, an exclusively sexual definition of love overlooks the essential nature of the bond of friendship. The underlying notion of love prevailing in that reading of your relationship is symptomatic of the dominant way of understanding love in my own time, and so I am not surprised that you and David are assumed to have been homosexual lovers. What particularly saddens me about the saturation of narratives equating sex with love in my culture (in movies, music, literature, and even school textbooks) is that it leaves no room for friendship, but rather sexualizes anything resembling human affection for a person, whether male or female.

A silly example of this comes to mind. A new term has been coined for a group of male friends who always hang out together: "bromance." Now, while the word is meant to be playful, it nevertheless suggests that male friendships need a sexual connotation, even if the relationship is not fueled by *eros*. A healthy attraction can and certainly does exist in friendship, but that does not by definition turn the friendship into a sexual one. Why can't a group of guys simply be allowed to enjoy the pleasure of each other's company and the shared interest or endeavor that unites them?

Another example perhaps illustrates my point better, even if you will probably have no idea what I am referring to. I read an article years ago which began with the author describing his experience in a theater watching one of *The Lord of the Rings* movies. In one scene, the heroes, Sam and Frodo, are shown embracing, with Sam then holding his friend's head after a very frail Frodo had just escaped certain death. The joy experienced by the characters upon rendezvousing after a frightful ordeal was evidently lost on a moviegoer sitting behind the author; he writes that he heard a voice snicker, "They must be gay!" as the scene unfolded.

I grant that these two examples hardly constitute proof of the reduction of *philia* to *eros*, or of friendship to homosexual love. But they are the logical byproduct, I think, of a frenzied and libertine sexual culture, daily bombarding us from our TVs and phones and computers (once again, you won't understand—human civilization waited until the twentieth century to enslave itself with image-producing machines). The confused uses of the word "love" common today have led to a widespread acceptance that anything is permitted to fall under the category of love so long as the lovers are honest and yield to the passions of their true selves. I fear that the super-sexed consequences of an anything-goes attitude toward love mark the end of friendship. I worry that the subtle elimination of friendship as an essential mark of human relationships is manifest in the homoerotic interpretation of your relationship with David. The two of you are often invoked as the "patron saints" of gay lovers, but if one reads your story with that lens, the value of committed friendship vanishes. It is one thing to distort a biblical story, but it is another thing entirely to reduce *philia* to *eros* on a culture-wide basis. Should that happen (and I think it is happening), there would be little incentive to commit (in the form of marriage vows) to a temporary feeling of love for any extended period of time, let alone for one's entire life. Love itself becomes simply a matter of convenience rather than the lifelong deepening of a bond, whether in friendship or in marriage. I don't want that to happen, Jonathan.

But at this point I'm simply rambling to myself. Let me finish by expressing my gratitude for your faithful commitment to David at a time in his life when he desperately needed a loyal friend. I read his eulogy of you as a sincere act of gratitude for your brotherly love. You provided him with a deep friendship that does not need to be romanticized in order to make us praise you. David clearly indulged in many empty erotic relationships; according to the biblical testimony, you might have been the only true male friend he ever had. He was surrounded by women and prophets and sons, but you were that unique friend who supported him in a time of trial as your father sought his life. I think your relationship shows that the cords of friendship, which form naturally among two males or two females and clearly bound the two of you together, pull people together chastely, without fear of being ridiculed, and provide a source of strength and even grace. Ideally, friends will be united ever more deeply in a trusting *philia* with the God of love, the God of *agape*, that highest form of love which purifies *eros* and elevates it beyond its lustful and selfish tendencies. To go through life (and to avoid the spears hurled by your father Saul!) without trusted friendships would be a great misfortune. I hope friendships such as that between you and David will not perish at the expense of "love" understood only in terms of sex.

Charles Carroll of Carrollton[1]

To the esteemed Charles Carroll of Carrollton,

The Declaration of Independence continues to be revered as the fundamental document proclaiming our nation's liberty, the enduring standard of freedom some 240 years after it was written. The boldness of the action detailed on that great parchment, the severance of all dependent ties with Great Britain, and the establishment of a new nation are reflected in the proud signatures listed at the bottom. Every schoolboy and girl in America recognizes the prominent handwriting of John Hancock occupying the central position. Looking at a copy of it, I recognize the names of those fathers whose memory burns brighter than the others, both on account of their merits and the favoritism of history: Benjamin Franklin, John Adams, Samuel Adams, and Thomas Jefferson among them.

I must confess, Mr. Carroll, that your name, listed with your fellow Maryland representatives below Mr. Hancock's autograph, never caught my attention as a youngster. History only allows a limited number of biographies to be hallowed through the centuries, and the choice of American heroes whose names remain on the lips of future generations is not always made according to objective criteria. Your contribution to the great cause of independence was totally unknown to me until very recently, but I have been extremely pleased to make your acquaintance, however tardily.

Catholics are often accused, sadly but truly so, of biblical illiteracy— that is, of being total ignoramuses with regard to the knowledge of Scripture. Catholics in America are guilty, I'm afraid, of an additional ignorance: that of their own history in this land of the free and home of the brave. A cursory glance at the map of the United States reveals the lasting influence

1. Charles Carroll of Carrollton (1737–1832) was the only Roman Catholic to sign the Declaration of Independence. He was also the first United States Senator from Maryland. For a helpful biography, see Birzer, *American Cicero*.

of the missionary Franciscans in places such as Florida, Texas, New Mexico, and California (many of California's largest cities began as missions, and retain the name of the mission's patron: San Diego, San Francisco, and so on). Some people might be aware of the Jesuit presence in the French territories such as Wisconsin and Illinois prior to American independence. But the manifest anti-Catholicism codified in many colonies, as well as your conspicuous role as a founding father of this beloved country, are sadly unknown to most Catholic Americans.

All papists living in the United States of America, in fact, owe an immense debt of gratitude to your entire family. Only recently did I learn that your cousin, John Carroll, was the first bishop appointed in the United States of America, with his see in Baltimore. No other Catholic family can claim such an essential position in the life of the American church for that reason alone, but you personally ensured that the Carrolls would long be praised for their courageous role in the political realm as well.

Your distinction as the last living signer of the Declaration of Independence is a happenstance honor that easily could have gone to another, as you surely acknowledged. Being the only Catholic to sign that noble document, however, is a highly worthy cause for acclaim. The fact that you argued courageously for independence in your beloved Maryland while unable to obtain full citizenship there on account of your profession of "Popery" is a testament to your perseverance in pursuit of a new birth of liberty. Earning the respect of patriots such as Benjamin Franklin and John Adams in spite of your papist leanings indicates your full commitment to the cause of independence. More importantly, though, it also makes clear that your support of religious toleration for all went hand in hand with the expectation that a self-governing people must be virtuous proponents of the common good for the new republic to have any chance of survival.

I am learning about your life, Mr. Carroll, at a most peculiar time in the history of the United States of America. You need not fear that a fight for independence or a second civil war of any sort is imminent, though you should ask your fellow Declaration signer Richard Henry Lee about his posterity's role in the first one! But I have had occasion to ponder the present political and moral situation in my beloved land in the light of your own life and writings, and I would simply like to share them, almost at random, with you in this letter. I don't mean to share my own peculiar political theory; such musings are beyond my ability to begin with, and I don't pretend to know the best form of government, nor would I be able to articulate such a position were I acquainted with it. I would rather inquire into your own reservations about democracy, especially the misgivings you voiced about the fledgling American project after General Washington's military triumph assured independence from the British king.

You wrote on several occasions, both in public letters and private correspondence, that you feared the push for democracy would descend into mob rule. If pure democracy won the day as the chosen form of government, you warned, a tyranny of the masses would soon replace the previous tyranny of a single monarch. Many of your contemporaries attributed your opinion to your own self-interest. As the wealthiest man in America and one at home in the aristocratic world of the British Empire, they contended that you were simply attempting to preserve your own massive advantages in trade and property. Many historians concur with this assessment of your motives, which would explain, at least in part, why you are not mentioned in the same breath as the other hallowed founding fathers.

I suppose self-interest is always mixed into even the most noble and altruistic of opinions; human beings of any time, after all, are naturally selfish creatures. But I think your worries stand on their own terms, regardless of your personal circumstances and influence. You saw quite clearly that democracy cannot be the rule of the simple majority. Were that form of rule to be established, government would essentially be reduced to a power-grab, with the victorious masses able to impose their will and even whims as law. You recognized the great need, as did many of your generation, for the separation of powers into the judicial, legislative, and executive, ensuring that no single branch of government would wield an excess of power. Just as important as this separation, though, was your insistence that the law of the new nation be grounded in the natural law, defended by pagans and Christians alike from Plato and Cicero to Augustine and Aquinas—that source of justice which originates with "nature and nature's God," and acts as the standard for the promotion and defense of the common good of a people in human precepts. You were aware that a people cannot self-govern if they do not govern themselves, that is, if they do not allow themselves to be ruled by any force other than their own passions, or any law not of their own capricious devising.

You feared, Mr. Carroll, that a democracy without the republican checks and balances would allow the leaders of that nation, and thus the people themselves, to embrace a different form of tyranny than the one they so recently had removed. The structure of our democratic republic, which you indirectly helped to craft and in which you served as the first Senator from Maryland, was a brilliant solution to secure liberty and justice for all, and to promote ways of correcting injustices in the future (I have in mind particularly the issues of slavery and rights for blacks and women).

As you pondered the proper form of government for our United States, Mr. Carroll, you surely assumed that the leaders enacting and enforcing laws would be models of virtue, regardless of their personal political preferences. The example of a leader sets the tone for the nation as a whole, and your generation produced such paragons as George Washington and John Adams, compelling profiles of wisdom, diplomacy, and magnanimity for future generations of leaders in America. Though they certainly have been lionized by the passage of time, and appear in almost legendarily reverent terms, they earnestly sought the common good of the thirteen colonies, and collaborated, despite differences of opinion, to form "a more perfect union." They were willing to set aside their own personal glory, however much that selfish desire might have animated their entrance into the battle for independence, for the greater good of the United States of America.

When I observe the political leaders of the present day, Mr. Carroll, and the nature of political life in the United States, I perceive a troubling contrast to your great generation of founding fathers. You feared the potential for chaos arising from pure democracy, in which the vulgar and unregulated masses take charge of those capable of ruling justly and effectively. But what if the politicians themselves are indistinguishable from the instinctively angry mob, manifestly craving power and conniving to grab and maintain it without thought for their example to others? What happens when political rhetoric descends to the level of schoolyard insults, and is treated by the complicit media as reality show entertainment?

Well, that seems to be precisely what we have today, Mr. Carroll. We are saturated by sound bites of candidates for the highest offices who are petulant power mongers. The classical definition of virtue as a formative principle of character for a nation and individuals dedicated to the common good seems to have become a *hindrance* to election. Sadly, though, those candidates apparently represent their desired constituencies accurately. When I examine the public discourse uttered in editorials, blogs, and articles, I hear cries of anger and egotism totally devoid of reason, fueled exclusively by emotional bombast. When I analyze appeals for rights, I hear precious little of corresponding duties to the state, which is designed to protect and promote those natural rights. Frankly, Mr. Carroll, I wonder if a nation whose foundations are pulverized by arbitrarily defined rights, and whose political leaders are consumed with the lust for power rather than love of country, can long endure.

Fear for the future is inevitable in every generation, yet seeds of hope are always planted, however small they may be or slowly they may grow. It is one thing, of course, to lament the present perceived malaise; but it is altogether more noble, as you and your generation of founders bore witness, to defend what has been entrusted to us, to forge bonds of peace and charity among our fellow Americans, and to seek a truly common good wherever we can, starting at the local levels of family, parish, city, county, and state.

I believe, Mr. Carroll, that American Catholics are in a unique position to accomplish this. We possess a solidly developed series of principles on social issues to draw from (broadly called Catholic Social Teaching), as well as our inherent desire for the health of the earthly city so that we may anticipate life in our heavenly homeland. My hope is that Catholics living in the United States would not be afraid to ennoble the public discourse by their words and friendships. I also greatly desire that Catholics would take an active and courageous role in government and positions of civic leadership. But all Catholic citizens should live in such a way that they remind their neighbors that our freedom gives us license to serve the Author of all law and to pursue what is eternally good and true, not to define what is true and good based on individual whims.

May American Catholics turn to you today, Mr. Carroll, for inspiration at this uncertain hour of our nation's life. May we pray with confidence that God, the author of our nature and the benevolent guide of all history, infuses the hearts of all Americans, and Catholics in particular, with the wisdom of past ages, the courage to change what we must, and a greater love of virtue to anchor us amid the vicissitudes of history.

Punxsutawney Phil[1]

To THE GREAT GROUNDHOG, Punxsutawney Phil, Seer of Seers and Prognosticator of Prognosticators,

The paltry words of human beings, as frail and fleeting in their momentary utterance as a cumulonimbus cloud, cannot possibly suffice to give proper homage to your most majestic and furry self. For more than 120 years, you, O most inscrutably wise marmot, universally hailed as "the Weatherman of the World," have held sway over clouds and seasons, determining when winter may pass on and spring may unfurl her warm and sunny banner upon our great globe. Every February the Second, your solemn high feast day, your courtiers rouse you from your (fake wooden tree-trunk) slumber spot at Gobbler's Knob, and wait to see whether you see your shadow stretching forth on that hallowed ground. The discernment of your shadow assures that six more weeks of long snowy winter loom before the vast populace; but should your regal body cast no dark hue on the ground, then rosy-fingered spring is guaranteed to come soon. Regardless of your prediction, always infallible, always just, all human pilgrims who gather in Punxsutawney, Pennsylvania for the sacred spectacle are grateful to catch a mere glimpse of your Phil-ness.

However unworthy I am to salute such an august member of the groundhog family, I proceed with the humble hope that you will deign to consider the thoughts expressed here as an ode to your inimitable awesomeness. May they be a consolation to you should you ever, in the dark of

---

1. Punxsutawney Phil is the beloved furry groundhog who dwells in Punxsutawney, Pennsylvania, and acts as the "weatherman of the world." Every Groundhog Day, February 2, Phil determines the future course of the elements: if he sees his shadow, six more weeks of winter are surely coming, but if he does not see his shadow, a sunny and pleasant spring is just around the corner.

your wintertime cave, be seized by a doubt (perish the thought!) that you are not properly adored by the general masses.

Your identity as the world's only marmot-meteorologist bestows on you tremendous and nearly unapproachable fame. Your status as an American icon has reached Hollywood (and therefore almost biblical) proportions. In what is now a classic comedy entitled *Groundhog Day*, Bill Murray portrays an egomaniac weatherman doomed to repeat February 2 over and over again. The film, a comic masterpiece, offers a profound meditation, influenced largely by Buddhist teachings on reincarnation and karma, on the difficulty and importance of conversion, or the purification of selfish desires to allow compassion toward others to govern one's life. My only complaint about the movie concerns a detail about which you are totally innocent, Phil. To my grandmother's great chagrin, not a single shot of *Groundhog Day* was actually filmed in Punxsutawney. I think some podunk town in Illinois received the honor of being a fake Punxsutawney for movie purposes. This manifest disgrace probably should prejudice my family's viewing of the movie, but its cinematic brilliance overcomes any lingering sense of scandal. At least when I'm in a forgiving mood.

But to return to the subject at hand, I will audaciously assert that I possess a special claim to your attention. I happen to have a fine family pedigree rooted in the very same soil you call home—except that my relatives live in houses. The great metropolis of Punxsutawney, Pennsylvania is the proud hometown of Grandma Esposito, numerous aunts, uncles, and cousins. My father was born and raised there, a proud graduate of Punxsutawney Area High School (home of the Chucks!), and Grandma has lived her entire life on Cherry Street, just a mile or so from the public library where you reside for most of the year, surrounded by Plexiglas to protect you from would-be assassins. She has admitted to me that she has frequented the hallowed woods of Gobbler's Knob only a handful of times in her life, and never on February 2, the day when the fate of the entire cosmos hinges on your infallible weather forecast. But she may be forgiven this minor offense, for her constant proximity to your sublime reality might obscure the radiant truth of your exalted nature.

I must, alas, make a confession of my own: I have never witnessed the revelry of February 2 at Gobbler's Knob firsthand either. I lived too far away in the shining paradise that is Omaha, Nebraska, and my teachers did not consider Groundhog Day an appropriate federal holiday worthy of a break from school. On the other hand, I have many wonderful recollections of

Punxsutawney from the summer months and Christmas time. My clearest memories of my grandfather are linked to baseball. He played catch with me and my brother in his backyard, and took us to several American Legion games at the nearby ball field. For his seventieth birthday, our family planned a surprise party for him, and his children and grandchildren wrote short notes on the keepsake tablecloth. I drew a Pittsburgh Pirates cap and a baseball, thanking him for sharing his love of the game with me. Less than a year later, my family and I returned for his funeral Mass.

My brother and I loved to walk down Cherry Street and meander downtown to the baseball card shop on Mahoning Street. The Chamber of Commerce was another favorite stop. It featured the latest Punxsutawney Phil memorabilia, with your whiskered face plastered on t-shirts, coffee mugs, hats, and golf balls. We were enthralled one summer by the Wild West exhibition put on as part of the Groundhog Festival, and I felt as though culture itself had died when a McDonald's was built on the spot where the saloon storefront had previously stood.

Nothing beat Christmas Eve dinner at Grandma's. Everyone in the area, including people I never knew were related to me, descended upon her happy home to enjoy her delicious pierogis, pizelles, and world-famous nutroll. The train Grandpa bought for my father and his siblings when they were children wound its way around the Christmas tree, and presents were greedily opened by cousins eager to help one another with the deconstruction of paper and boxes. Some of us would then dress up all fancy-like and go to Saints Cosmas and Damian down the road for Midnight Mass. Afterward, my family and I would retire to the Groundhog Motel, since all of Grandma's rooms were occupied by other relatives.

For all these geographical and familial connections binding me to you, Phil, they are supplemented by an even greater marvel, one made possible by the blessed gift of taxidermy. Sometime in my middle school years, the Esposito clan in Omaha received a large brown box from an unknown Punxsutawney address. As I stood in the kitchen eating an after-school snack, I heard hysterical shrieks from another room as my mother pulled out a giant stuffed rodent from the styrofoam packaging. An accompanying letter from my great-uncle revealed that he had graciously bestowed upon us a real (if dead) Punxsutawney Phil—an essential link in the dynastic chain of Groundhogs! This particular Phil, surely a direct ancestor of yours, was active in the 1950s, and is now immortally stuffed and permanently affixed to a wooden post.

The beautiful creature is posed on his hind legs, and stands about two and a half feet tall. I found this to be quite unnatural, but it creates a more dramatic effect on the observer ignorant of rodent motion. His finely combed tail (and the clearly visible wire attached to it) juts out gently from his frame. His fur, oh so soft and cuddly, was the recipient of endless loving strokes by myself and my siblings for many years. His right arm is gracefully extended as though in benediction, and his index "finger" and nail point proudly to the stars, his buck teeth flashing a smile one can only call imperial but benevolent. A strange cut near his nose led me to believe that he had been shot, perhaps in a publicity dispute with his cruel human handlers. Whatever the cause of his death might have been, the Esposito family was thrilled to have this Punxsy Phil all to ourselves. Though we knew ourselves to be unworthy of such a gift, we provided him (and honored you, by extension) with the adoring affection his dignitary status deserved. He was, you may be sure, the star of several unforgettable show-and-tells at school. This family heirloom later made the trek to college with me for my final semesters, and was the centerpiece of my apartment living room. I purchased a circular red and gold amulet from Goodwill for him to wear daily, as a reminder of his innate regality to all who frequented our pad either to venerate his relics, or to be shocked at the presence of a rodent in human living quarters.

Phil, you may have your detractors and cheap imitators, and Punxsutawney may be a small town ignored by most people 364 days of the year, but I take great pride in my family roots there. The goodness of small-town America is evident in the friendliness of the people there, the simplicity of their lives, and the joy they receive from humorous events such as Groundhog Day. The inhabitants of every town and state find their own claim to fame, highlighting their boast of being the first or best at something, or being the hometown of a famous athlete or politician. Groundhog Day, to me, is certainly a quirky festival producing a (forgive me for saying this) dubious weather forecast—but it is good to be recognized by non-locals for something pleasant and innocent such as this. I suspect that it is a rallying point of pride for the locals too, even if many of them, like Grandma Esposito, don't flock to Gobbler's Knob in the early morning hours of February 2 to freeze while waiting for your two minutes of public spectacle.

Perhaps my early experiences in Punxsutawney predisposed me to think less of big towns when I grew up. I find large American cities to be cold—full of impressive buildings, landscapes, and art to be sure, but lacking in personality, and unable to generate a feeling of connectedness among those living there. Though I live near a big city, my monastery is sufficiently isolated to offer a sense of detachment from the hustle and bustle of Dallas. Strangely enough, Punxsutawney comes to mind whenever I think of a phrase used to describe Saint Alberic, one of the founders of the Cistercian Order to which I belong. One of his fellow monks described him, among other saintly attributes, as an *amator loci*, a "lover of the place" where his monastery was located. Saint Alberic's love of place rooted him to that particular monastery, and he never desired to move anywhere else. I committed my life to my monastery by making a vow of stability, voluntarily rooting myself to this particular place, and I find that my own love of this Cistercian Abbey attracts people who do not have such an attachment or commitment to a particular place or family. Perhaps a love for a specific spot, especially one from childhood, could draw someone perpetually rootless, traveling for work and longing for a break, back to the stability and security they lack at present. Perhaps a man or woman who has nothing to get excited about in the humdrum of corporate life in a grey skyscraper can smile in anticipation of a silly community-bonding experience such as Groundhog Day. Perhaps they will return home for the first time in a long while and rekindle a love of family that had grown cold, whether by accident or painful incident. Perhaps they will pray in a church whose sturdy walls provide a sense of comfort and community thanks to the liturgy, recalling that Jesus spent his early years in a small town surrounded by family.

Should I ever get the chance to return to Punxsutawney, good Phil, I will not fail to salute you from your glass cave at the public library. If you are hibernating, I will make every attempt to startle you awake, and I will personally hand you a copy of this letter if I manage to elude the security forces surrounding your abode. You may do with it as your regal rodent majesty wishes, but I will be humbly honored just to cross "letting the Groundhog personally know I am a loyal fan/subject" off my bucket list!

Saint Bernadette[1]

DEAR BERNADETTE,

Providence is a more fitting word than coincidence to describe an attraction to a particular saint. I regard my connection to you as natural and predestined, but in the happy sort of way: with both a grandmother and a mother named after you, I made your acquaintance quite early in life, and thoughts of you have never been far from my mind. I came to realize that my link to you was even further well-fated when I joined my Cistercian abbey. Your name, of course, was patterned after that of Saint Bernard of Clairvaux, the great Cistercian and Doctor of the Church, so I have multiple patronages (and French ones at that!) to be grateful for.

I recall my mom speaking about you and the Lourdes grotto on many occasions. Her fervent love of Mary, the mother of Jesus, was (and continues to be) greatly aided by your intercessory role in her life. One particular description of the lady who appeared to you in the Massabielle grotto captivated my mom, and she often repeated it in our presence: "Saint Bernadette said that the lady was so beautiful that you would willingly die to see her again!"

I was the first person in my family to make a pilgrimage to Lourdes. I arrived, at the beginning of a frigid new year, with four college classmates, having made absolutely no provisions for lodging (because why bother planning *before* you travel to a totally unfamiliar place?). Virtually every hostel was shuttered for the non-tourist season, and only the generous pity of a small group of nuns secured us a warm place to sleep for several days. Given the wretched January weather, we did not encounter the crowded

1. Saint Bernadette Soubirous (1844–1879) was a young girl in Lourdes, France when the Blessed Virgin Mary appeared to her numerous times in a grotto. Lourdes has since become a place of pilgrimage attracting millions of people annually, many of whom hope for a physical cure by bathing in the waters of the grotto.

masses of pilgrims, sick and healthy, which are found during the peak months. One afternoon was particularly memorable: a gentle but steady blizzard blanketed the entire place, and I took a graced and wonderful stroll along the Via Crucis, the path and statues alike all covered by a soft layer of snow. I plunged myself into the chilly waters of the grotto, and after being fully immersed, I recall marveling that I did not feel cold and, stranger still, needed no towel to dry off. I suppose this letter to you can act as a small gesture of my gratitude for the grace that flowed to me at that blessed spot.

I have returned to your story on multiple occasions since my pilgrimage to Lourdes. As a novice in my monastery, I was asked to make presentations on two saints over the course of the year. The first was my patron, Thomas More, and you were the second. I devoured several books about you, and particularly enjoyed a biography by René Laurentin entitled *Bernadette of Lourdes*. A few years later, I delighted in the novel of your life called *The Song of Bernadette*, written by Franz Werfel, one of my favorite authors. Werfel was a German Jew who fled the Nazis in 1940. He and his wife found refuge in Lourdes for several months, and there learned about your story. He made a vow that if he successfully escaped the Nazi clutches, he would celebrate your life by writing about it. He fulfilled his pledge when he came to America. The novel is a masterpiece.

But the preceding paragraphs have all been introductory and formal. The lady, Bernadette—I want to talk to you about the lady. That was the way you constantly described the woman who appeared to you in the niche of the grotto. Near the end of the apparitions, she revealed a name, or perhaps a title, by which she would be known, but your simple humility prevented you from asserting outright that the Virgin Mary was the woman gracing you with her unique presence. Theologians immediately commented that the name the lady shared with you, "the Immaculate Conception," confirmed in a most radical way the Pope's declaration of that very dogma only four years before the apparitions. After a grueling number of years featuring interminable interviews, vocal skeptics, and increasing numbers of miraculous healings at the grotto, the bishop of Lourdes declared your visions to be authentic Marian apparitions. By that time, though, you had already retreated into the silence of your cloister in Nevers, a place I still wish to visit.

During one of the first apparitions, the lady delivered a harsh pledge to you: "I do not promise to make you happy in this world, but in the next." This statement, Bernadette, troubles many people. It seems to reinforce a persistent criticism leveled against the Catholic faith in your nineteenth-century France, and one still voiced in my twenty-first century. Opponents of the faith, especially Communists in your day and radical atheists in mine, accuse Christianity of creating an illusory dream-world called heaven for the poor and sick to long for, so that they won't attempt to fix their miserable earthly condition. The church, supposedly the great enemy of material progress, desperately tries to maintain its authority over the ignorant masses by any means necessary, and prevents social change in the process. As you painfully realized, Bernadette, your simple peasant faith was ridiculed by the enlightened intelligentsia of your day. In the eyes of many, the lady's instructions only legitimized their rejection of a superstitious religion which dares to assert that miracles can occur within the realm of nature.

Your discovery of grotto water producing sudden and lasting cures of terrible illnesses brought great notoriety to Lourdes, but objectors still maintained the absurdity of the situation. An argument such as the following is frequently voiced regarding Lourdes and, indirectly, the Christian faith as a whole: "Good for those people who claim to be healed in ways modern science cannot explain by bathing in or drinking the grotto water. But the pilgrim flocks who converge on Lourdes by the millions ignore the fact that the lady didn't cure suffering. Unjust misery still manifestly afflicts a huge percentage of the globe, and Bernadette and her lady can't, *and God Almighty apparently doesn't want to*, do anything about it!"

In point of fact, Bernadette, the blessed Virgin did not lie to you. Just as your early years were marked by poverty and sickness, your final years in the convent were a perpetual agony of physical pain and frequent spiritual desolation. I cannot pose the question, "Was all your earthly suffering worth it?" because I believe, as you did, that you had an eternal reward waiting for you on the other side of death's curtain, the very promise of beatitude indicated to you by the lady.

But I do want to ask you how we can make some sense of suffering here on earth. While the thrill of freedom can somehow taste sweeter once a cruel dictator is overthrown, or a cure for cancer can bring new hope to thousands afflicted with that disease, it is hard to find any redeeming purpose for suffering without recourse to an eternal promise of bliss. Contrary to the Communist rhetoric of Marx and others, the specter of heaven does not for a moment excuse Christians from securing social justice for the poor, the sick, and the marginalized. We simply cannot, however, expect that a perfectly happy and just society will ever flourish, given the material that society must be built with.

That material is the human being, capable of immense sacrificial love and the most callous and terrifying violence. Many forms of suffering, Bernadette, are the product of humanity's monstrous selfishness—that is to say, sin. In this context, I recall that the lady often spoke the word "penance" to you, as well as the injunction to pray for sinners. That message, frankly, seems little more than a disappointing letdown. There is no promise to end pain, suffering, or death, and no pledge to eradicate evil from the world. The lady offers only a counsel of prayer, a vague course of action which only a select few souls, such as yourself, consider in any way desirable or even remotely fruitful.

Yet her message is not a new one. The very origin of the Christian faith, after all, lies in the act of an innocent man bearing the burdens of those who could not bear them. Yes, God allows suffering, and it bothers me that I can't give a reasonable explanation for its persistence, especially when innocent and good people are ravaged by disease or poverty. You surely have a comprehension of the divine plan from your heavenly vantage point, one that is off limits to us. But we know that God has identified with those suffering, the poor in spirit, in Christ. By his willingness to assume all the limitations of human existence, he came to know by experience our mortal reality. By his death on the cross, he accepted on his shoulders all the violence and senseless suffering heaped up by humanity in every generation. By his act of selfless love, his outstretched arms embrace us, receive our punishable guilt, and remind us that he has undone the bonds of suffering and death so that they cannot ultimately triumph over us.

But even with that understanding of God's willingness to share our sorrows and infirmities, Bernadette, I cannot justify the misery of the human condition simply by voicing some soothing theological truths, or in any way rejoice in that misery. Perhaps some consolation is available when we realize that misery makes possible an outpouring of God's mercy. In Latin, the word for mercy, *misericordia*, contains within its very root the term *miseria*. That actually gives me a possible insight into the reason for the many Marian apparitions in recent centuries. Your lady was at the foot of the cross as her son conquered death by his own death. As a result, she possesses a profound understanding of the suffering men and women must endure in this world. Her maternal capacity for suffering with them, and for providing constant consolation, just might be what humanity needs most at this point in history. Rather than removing the focus from Jesus, proper devotion to Mary allows us to view her son as she does, and draws us ever closer to his loving arms.

All of this, though, is sheer brain-think on my part. I am constantly blown away by the confident trust exhibited by friends and strangers who struggle with chronic and life-threatening illnesses. By their words, they express an amazing conviction that their suffering is somehow a gift they can return to God. I have often made sense of their displays of faith by thinking that they are bearing the burdens which people of weaker faith could not possibly bear. In that way, sick and innocent sufferers (such as yourself) are like the spiritual Atlases of the world. You endure physical and spiritual sorrows so that others don't have to.

To that end, I want to share with you the words of a dear friend of mine. His name is Daniel Pruit, and he has endured for many years a disease called cystic fibrosis. As the disease was ravaging his lungs, Daniel, now twenty-five, expressed an unshakeable certainty that his suffering was not absurd. He taught his theology teachers about the nature of love and perseverance in blog posts such as the following:

> I don't fully understand the mystery that is "redemptive suffering," but I do know that it gives tremendous value to something that would otherwise be meaningless. I like to think of it in an analogy. Graphite (the stuff in your pencil) and diamonds (the most beautiful and expensive gem) share a common characteristic. They are both pure carbon. What distinguishes the two is their molecular makeup. Graphite is composed of layers of molecules, whereas diamonds are cubic in nature. When put under high temperatures and incredible pressure, graphite molecules are forced to re-align and form a cubic formation known as crystal, and a diamond is born. Through his awesome power, God is capable of turning something like graphite into diamond . . . Diamonds are made only by applying intense pressure and heat over a long period of time, and love can only be proven through intense and prolonged sacrifice . . .
>
> Just as both are made of pure carbon, my body has been made to suffer from this disease whether I like it or not, so I might as well offer it to God and let Him re-align it and give it a purpose. If (through mother nature) He can turn graphite into diamonds on a physical level, think of how much more He can do with suffering on a spiritual level!

How God uses my CF is a mystery, no doubt, but what He did on the Cross gives me solace when my willpower is completely spent. All I have to do is look at a Crucifix to see the efficacious model of redemption through pain. It renews my energy and zeal for fighting CF, and assures me that all of my frustration with this disease is being used as spiritual ammo for God and His servants. This faith in Christ's Cross has been inspiring people for 2,000 years. It is truly a "gift that keeps on giving," and it's one of those things that no one can take away from a person. Faith and hope come from knowledge of the infinite goodness of God, not from anything earthly, and this is why one can be joyful in the midst of terrible sickness. As Philippians 4:6–7 says, "Be anxious for nothing, but in everything by prayer and supplication, with thanksgiving, let your requests be made known to God; and the peace of God, which surpasses all understanding, will guard your hearts and minds through Christ Jesus." Real faith requires being unafraid of vulnerability and weakness, and an uncomfortable amount of humiliation, but if you trust in God, the reward of your faith will be this incredible inner peace . . .

[Heaven] is not a place in the clouds, or a myth created to make people feel better about dying. Heaven means being in a state of full communion with God, who created us and knows everything we have ever thought or done, and yet who loves us infinitely. The peace that comes from knowing you are doing God's Will is a little slice of heaven. Heaven is also eternal. It has *no end*, which is a mind-boggling concept on its own. The more you think about that, the shorter your earthly life gets, and the more serious Jesus' call to "take up your cross and follow me" gets. It should give us great hope and joy, and give us the strength to "seize the day" even when we are suffering and in a lot of pain. I think about heaven a lot and how awesome it's gonna be, but I'm in no hurry to get there. For now, I'll just try and unite my sufferings with His, stay close to Him in the sacraments, and remember that no matter what happens, God's got this!"[2]

Daniel received a double lung transplant in the summer of 2015. For years prior to his surgery, he needed an oxygen tank and could barely walk more than five minutes without losing his breath. Just months after receiving his new lungs, he sprinted to the top of a 13,000-foot mountain. Though his cystic fibrosis is still lurking, his heart is too full of gratitude to worry

2. This excerpt is taken from the November 28, 2013 entry on Daniel's blog: https://danielpruit.wordpress.com/author/dpruit/

about what comes next. His testimony reveals that human reason, cold to the touch of divine love, cannot perceive what the logic of faith recognizes. Daniel was recently selected to go on pilgrimage to Lourdes, and he asked me to accompany him. The awareness of the thinness of the space, or rather his sense that the barrier between heaven and earth is almost transparent at that beautiful sanctuary, brought forth from his lungs deep breaths of gratitude and cries of joy to be able to pray there. What he found at Lourdes was, I believe, a beautiful foretaste of the eternal healing awaiting him at the end of his race, as well as a greater friendship with you and reliance on your prayers!

Lyle Alzado[1]

Dear Lyle,

Weekly issues of *Sports Illustrated* formed the bulk of my reading material as a young boy. I yearned to get home from school on Thursdays so I could devour the contents of the latest edition that had just arrived in the mail. My favorite reading spot, to be honest, was the toilet, that glorious man-throne where I could quite easily spend an hour lost in the happy perusal of my favorite magazine from beginning to end. The glossy photos of athletes I idolized, the host of statistics, news, and fascinating stories, all combined to make sports an essential part of my childhood. My fascination with all things related to sports continues to this day, even if I have to moderate it so as not to detract from doing the monk-thing as best I can!

I remember your picture on the cover of *SI* when I was eight years old or so. Your fierce scowl and angry protruding jaw, the bane of NFL quarterbacks for many years, were complemented by a black bandana on your head with red skulls. The headline was even more startling than your scary stare: "I LIED." The smaller print underneath contained the strange word "steroids."

At the time, I was too young to fully grasp the confession you made in the lead article. I simply thought it was sad that you, a terror of a defensive end, were dying of brain cancer just a few years after you retired. As an adult, I now have a sense of the tragic retrospective you offered to *SI* about your maniacal use of steroids. I found that article online recently, and reread it with great sorrow. I admired your honesty as you admitted to lying about your use of anabolic steroids and, during a short-lived comeback

1. Lyle Alzado (1949–1992) was a defensive end in the National Football League, playing for the Denver Broncos, Cleveland Browns, and Los Angeles Raiders. He died of a brain tumor, and was convinced that his constant use of anabolic steroids was the cause of the fatal tumor.

attempt, human growth hormone. You vividly outlined the reasons why you began to use them, why you never stopped using them, and why you firmly believed that they caused the brain cancer which would kill you at the age of forty-three.

By your own admission, Lyle, you needed the boost in muscle mass to get bigger, to earn playing time, and to acquire that competitive edge which allowed you to excel. Your performance on the gridiron, where you were known for your reckless violence, earned you a handful of All-Pro selections and a Super Bowl ring with the Raiders. You enjoyed a career almost any defensive lineman would envy. Yet one sentence was all you needed to sum up your football career and the endless cycle of drugs which made it possible: "It wasn't worth it." You recognized that you could boast of solid career statistics, especially quarterback sacks, but you invited people to look at your ravaged body and observe the price you paid for your football glory and respectable numbers.

Your story was, in a real sense, only the first chapter of a troubling narrative that continues to be written and does not have an obvious end in sight. A few years after you died, *SI* featured another cover story devoted to steroids. The front image of that issue is indelibly etched in my head: a massive arm, flexing a smooth and bulging bicep, holds a needle and loaded syringe placed tenderly between the wrist and the bicep. The headline read "Bigger, Stronger, Faster." The article treated the widespread use of performance-enhancing drugs among Olympic athletes, as well as the lack of effective detection methods and punishments coming from national team and Olympic officials for users testing positive.

My main recollection of that article was a poll taken of roughly 200 Olympic athletes who responded honestly (and, of course, anonymously) to questions about their attitude toward steroids. When asked if they would take a banned substance with the assurance that they would not get caught and that the drug would guarantee them a gold medal, all but three said yes. The answers given to the next survey question were even more drastic: when asked if they would take a banned performance-enhancing substance that would guarantee them a gold medal *and* kill them soon after from its side effects, *more than half of the athletes said yes.*

Those responses still haunt me even if they don't surprise, given the exposés of steroid use in sports over the last twenty years. You certainly would not be shocked at those numbers. In your confession, you speculated that the number of NFL players on performance-enhancing drugs was around 90 percent, and that almost everyone you knew in football was taking something. You didn't live to see the lid of secrecy lifted on the use of drugs, as well as the uncovering of the willful ignorance on the part of player unions and international officials spanning many athletic boundaries to address the epidemic silently dominating the world of sports.

The epicenter of the steroids scandal, at least in the United States, was baseball. Yet another *SI* cover story in 2002 threw the game's secret out in the open thanks to a courageous journalist and his work with one retired ballplayer, Ken Caminiti. Ken was the 1996 National League MVP while playing for the Padres, and he described how steroids enabled him to have the career year he did. Unlike you, his confession did not include any form of apology at all. He insisted that the drugs were necessary for him to compete at the Major League level, even if his desire to excel required him to become a theorist in biochemical chaos. Several other players interviewed for the article complained anonymously that by remaining clean, they put themselves at a competitive disadvantage on the baseball diamond.

The cover of that issue features a glowing baseball behind two needle-and-syringe combos crossing each other. The story of widespread steroid use, long known in clubhouses but never confronted in public, finally came out. The "juiced ball" era became the dominant narrative, casting a dark shadow over the game. It has led to asterisks on home run records, deliberate exclusion of the most prominent juicers from the Hall of Fame, and obligatory testing for all baseball players. Some good has clearly come from the whistleblowing that took place. But I bring up the case of baseball here, Lyle, primarily because Ken Caminiti met the same fate you did: an early death, likely hastened by irresponsible and fanatical steroid use.

I don't mean to give the impression that the baseball scandal resolved the problem, whether in baseball itself or across the sports spectrum. Far from it—lab techs and scientists are continuously one step ahead of the testers, and investigations continue to reveal scandals, whether in cycling (Lance Armstrong, Floyd Landis), track and field (Marion Jones and the Russians banned from competing in the Rio Olympics), and football (too many culpables to list). Every world record, every stupendous athletic achievement, now comes saddled with doubts about how that accomplishment came about.

During the height of the baseball scandal, many fans and journalists lodged complaints against the athletes who voluntarily turned themselves into pharmacological labs, blending unregulated and illegal drugs and craving any substance that would provide them with the strength, the body, the speed they needed to achieve their dreams. The protests mostly revolved around the damage done to "the purity of the game," or "a loss of innocence" in the national pastime. These objections certainly come from noble sentiments and righteous outrage, and they reflect the sadness stemming from the knowledge that humans have willingly turned themselves into freaky, muscle-strapped Frankensteins to produce the home runs and superhuman highlights we so love to admire.

But such sentiments avoid the deeper and more disconcerting philosophical question involved in all of this. There seems to be both a fundamental misunderstanding of the purpose of sport and an obscuring of the very meaning of being human that saturate the mindset of the athletes who play the games we love. I totally understand the desire to get bigger and stronger, to make up for athletic deficiencies in order to make the team, or move from benchwarmer to starter, or from a productive player to an All-Star. I myself was never tempted to dope or take steroids, mostly because I was a skinny runner who knew his athletic limits and was content simply to compete and enjoy the camaraderie of teammates. But that innate thirst for glory, for victory at any cost, as you mentioned in your confession, has always been a hallmark of the human psyche. Achilles and his thirst for glory, whether on the running track or the field of battle, is the great archetype of this relentless quest. It was already manifest in the earliest athletic competitions, such as the original Olympic games, and has been transmitted to us in the great poetic praises sung of the Greek champions. The desire for a competitive edge and the willingness to cheat in order to attain victory are, I imagine, nothing new.

But you bravely raised the question about the cost of this uninhibited hunger for victory, as well as the attitude toward the human body and the human spirit required to endure the consequences of training and taking. In short, Lyle, I think your generation and mine both have a terribly flawed perception of nature and the body. What nature has given us in the form of the human body and its ability to be trained for awe-inspiring athletic feats is clearly regarded as insufficient by those who rely on steroids. Nature is just not enough, and the drive for enhanced performance, regardless of the sport, truly has no ultimate end or goal besides greater progress, lower world-record times, and more eye-popping stats. The only difference between us and the ancients on this score, of course, is that our pharmaceutical genius can contribute far more to an enhanced performance. It can also kill us.

And that is scary—not because I am averse to seeing hallowed records fall, but because so many people regard the value of their life solely in terms of what they do with, and to, their body. There is a certain desperation which goes hand-in-hand with steroid use, and is clearly reflected in the poll I mentioned above: more than half of the Olympic athletes surveyed hold that nothing greater can be achieved in life than a gold medal, and that death is welcome provided that they have their athletic glory (once again, the Achilles complex). To achieve that glory, nothing is off limits to these athletes, to the extreme point that even the distortion and destruction of their physical bodies become acceptable means, as long as the end of victory is met. The spiritual poverty of our time, indeed the perennial human temptation to a fatalistic understanding of this mortal life, is strikingly evident here.

Perhaps *the* original sin of pride plays out in athletic terms right here, for it reveals to us the seemingly innate and craven desire to be godlike, *to be someone we are not*, and to strive for the immortal glory that we cannot hold forever. That desire leads us to consider life not worth living if we cannot win a crown of olive wreaths, or a medallion of gold that can be placed in a drawer and forgotten. Even the honor granted the original Olympic winners, an ode written by the great Pindar, has little value to the victor when he has returned to the dust from which he came.

Lyle, are we less human if we refuse to succumb to the temptation to fabricate ourselves into something we are not? It's bad enough that you and Ken Caminiti do not deter more athletes and individuals from using drugs, but I worry that a disgraceful mindset has taken root in American society as a result of 'roid rage. It is one which willingly tolerates the pushing of human boundaries *as long as the public is entertained and money is generated*, and which looks the other way as our humanity is reduced to what we can do to our bodies. With this mindset so ingrained in children, let alone adults, no thought can possibly be given to the possible ends of a human life greater than physical achievements, or the possible reasons why we received our bodies as a blessing in the first place.

Perhaps I am being too dramatic in thinking that our humanity is at stake in this debate. Maybe I should welcome the genetic testing and chemical manipulations which promise to improve our speed, reaction time, strength, and endurance. Yet, having written that, maybe I shouldn't entertain the legitimacy of eugenics, given the consequences of such efforts already seared on the human psyche in the last century. I do wonder, though, why the vocal objectors defending nature from the syringe still insist on the need to be clean. Where does that desire to play fair come from? Could it be a check on our inhumanity, an innate response to the perpetual temptation to self-divinization at the expense of others created, as we are, in the image of Someone who does not think that human flourishing requires a gold medal?

My hope, Lyle, is that the warning of your death, as well as the caution of sensible and reflective people, would restart a conversation about the ends for which human beings were created, and the damage done if we reduce the human being to a physical specimen capable of being violated for mere entertainment and the vain pursuit of fleeting glory.

Barabbas[1]

Dear Barabbas,

Murder, robbery, and sedition, however newsworthy they might be, are not sufficient by themselves to keep the name of the criminal committing them alive on the lips of history. Much depends, of course, on *who* was murdered, *what* was stolen, and *which* revolution was instigated. Some murderers, thieves, and outlaws may gain notoriety during their time living on the lam, but the deed itself is more likely to be remembered than the name of the offenders. Their names surely pass into oblivion after a few generations have had time to forget the event.

Not so with you, Barabbas. Though the precise nature of your criminal activity is uncertain, your name has been preserved by texts called Gospels, and is uttered at a specific point in the liturgical year of a religion you knew nothing about. Your name, in the Aramaic tongue you spoke, means "son of the father"—ironic to be sure, since you are known today solely on account of your encounter with the Son of a very different Father.

I learned about you from the books Christians such as myself venerate because they contain selections of the words and deeds of a man I will speak of soon. You had been imprisoned by the Romans for some riotous behavior. One of the Gospel writers simply refers to you as "notorious," and another as a bandit, while two others identify you as a participant in a rebellion and a killer. You were detained in Jerusalem, where you were presumably to be tried and sentenced to a just and vicious death. Near the Jewish feast of Passover, the Roman procurator, Pontius Pilate, had a custom of releasing one prisoner to the Jews in honor of their religious celebration. His motivation might have been to mollify the antagonism of the Jews

---

1. Barabbas was a violent criminal released instead of Jesus by Pontius Pilate, a scene narrated in all four Gospels.

toward the foreign rulers of their land. You may have been one such zealous member of the people of Israel who despised their Roman occupiers, and channeled your hatred into violent and deadly acts of protest.

If so, you would not have been an ideal candidate for the honor of being freed by the Roman procurator, whose sole job was to ensure the peace bestowed on the world by the Empire. Yet, one Friday morning before Passover, Pilate, seated on his judgment bench in the Roman building known as the *praetorium*, granted the request of the Jews assembled there to release you. According to the Gospel accounts, your popularity with the people did not bring about your liberation. You were chosen, rather, to be liberated in preference to someone else.

The man's name was Jesus, and he was from Nazareth. He had been arrested the previous evening, betrayed by one of his disciples to the senior Jewish authorities. Pilate heard the accusations brought against him: blasphemous talk of his claiming to be "the Son of Man," of his supernatural power, of a kingdom not of this world, of the title "Messiah" or "Christ" being applied to him. He did not find, however, any evidence worthy of a death sentence. He protested the innocence of the man and wished to set him free, but the leaders of the people in Jerusalem managed to sway first the crowd and then Pilate himself to order his crucifixion. According to the evangelist Matthew, Pilate offered the people a choice between yourself and Jesus. The other three evangelists suggest that the crowd, instigated by the chief priests, yelled out your name as the favored one to receive the procurator's mercy:

> The procurator again said to them, "Which of the two do you want me to release for you?" They said, "Barabbas." (Matt 27:21)

> The crowd came forward and began asking him to do as he had previously done for them. Pilate answered them, "Do you want me to release for you the King of the Jews?" For he knew that the chief priests had handed him over out of envy. But the chief priests incited the crowd to have him release Barabbas for them instead. (Mark 15:8–11)

> But they were all crying out together, saying, "Take this one away! Release Barabbas for us!" (Luke 23:18)

> "But there is a custom among you that I release one person for you at Passover; do you want me to release for you the King of the Jews?" They cried out again, "Not this one, but Barabbas." (John 18:39–40)

As part of the arrangement, Pilate asked what was to be done about Jesus, whom he identified as "the king of the Jews." The response of the bloodthirsty crowd was seemingly unanimous: "Crucify him!" In virtually the same minute that you gained your freedom, Jesus earned the condemnation of a wretched death. After Pilate released you, he ordered Jesus to be scourged, and then his long, cross-burdened ascent to Golgotha began.

I presume that you at least laid your eyes on the man who received the death sentence. What must have passed through Jesus' mind as he, the Son who spoke so frequently of his relationship with his Father, stood condemned while you, Barabbas, "son of the father," walked away unshackled by cross or chain? The Gospels do not explicitly state that you were present at this exchange, but it is reasonable to think that you had the opportunity to look upon the one who would be crucified and "pierced for our transgressions," to quote the prophet Isaiah. You surely did not realize at the time, and perhaps you never came to understand, that you were the first recipient of the gift he bestowed upon all humanity by his crucifixion. The fact that he, not you, was condemned by Pilate means that, in a very real sense, he died for you, granting you a literal lease on life before his agonizing end on Calvary conferred spiritual life on all others.

As recorded and known to history, your life ends with your release. I initially decided to write to you because I have pondered what became of you after that Good Friday encounter, and I want to know the rest of your story. As a child, I formed an impression of you as a raging zealot lacking any semblance of intelligence, a born bandit with an irascible appetite for destruction. I always assumed that you returned to your rowdy and homicidal ways after Pilate acquitted you, and that you even took the Roman pardon as a further insult which intensified your loathing for the dirty Gentiles dominating your people and your land.

But I recently read a stunning book about your life after the acquittal that offered a very different perspective from the one I had adopted until now. The book, bearing the simple title *Barabbas*, was written by a Swedish author named Pär Lagerkvist, who won the Nobel Prize for literature in 1951. Though the story is purely a work of fiction, I love how the author envisioned the unfolding of your life after your encounter with Christ, and for the sake of this letter I will assume that the fictional account of you is true. The work is an outstanding piece of literature, and I don't want to steal the pleasure of reading it from you, so I won't offer too many spoilers here. But I can't resist commenting on a few scenes!

After Pilate releases you and initiates the execution process for Jesus, you feel compelled to witness the final moments of Jesus' earthly life on Golgotha, and you also stand before the empty tomb on Easter Sunday. What motivates you to follow these momentous events is left unsaid, but you clearly were trying to make sense of the encounter with the man who was condemned in conjunction with your acquittal. You meet many of his followers, though only Peter treats you with any compassion, and you, an unloved and solitary vagabond all your life, fail to grasp the phrase "Love one another" repeated frequently throughout the book.

At bottom, you are unable to reconcile the suffering which God evidently required with the command to love: not only the sacrifice of Jesus on the cross, but also the persecution and daily threat of martyrdom confronting the first Christians in Jerusalem and the various parts of the Roman Empire, seem impossible to accept. In a beautifully symbolic image, you wear a disk around your neck with the name "Jesus Christ" scratched onto it by a devout Christian whom you meet, but the name is later crossed out roughly. When forced to admit whether you are a Christian to a Roman governor, you tell him that you have no god, but you also confess that you want to believe, in response to his question about the name inscribed on the disk.

The final scene of the book depicts your last days and the hour of your death, brought about in Rome as the author connects your presence there with the famous citywide fire that Nero blamed on the Christians in AD 64. You suffer the same death as the man whose condemnation brought about your freedom, and you utter a sentence that brilliantly tugs the reader toward both belief and unbelief. Do you entrust your soul to God at the last instance like the good thief next to Christ, or do you give up the ghost to the darkness enveloping you? The ending is ambiguous, though I have a definite opinion on your intention behind the phrase.

Barabbas, I was grateful to Lagerkvist for offering me a renewed chance to think about you. He offered me ample space for reflection as I pondered his configuration of what your life could have looked like after a Good Friday meeting with the person I call "my Lord and my God." While you could very well have returned to your marauding ways without a second thought for the criminal about to be executed, I am inclined to think that your eye contact with Jesus, however brief, gave you pause at some point in your life (whether immediately or later), and prompted you to investigate the claims of that man and his disciples.

What fascinates me most about your life as presented in Lagerkvist's book is that your character, so coldly isolated from all genuine love your entire life, nevertheless *wants* to believe that the suffering of Jesus is not absurd, that the love his followers preach is the authentic means of encountering God. Yours is a character that, I think, is terribly common in my own day, where a great multitude of women and men made for communion with God desire the ability to believe, but fail to understand how to love, and never learn to seek God properly. They are not helped in their search, of course, by the dismissive and angry judgments of those who do claim to love and possess true belief, much as the Christian disciples in Lagerkvist's book scorn you once they recognize you as the one acquitted at the expense of Jesus.

My hope for those like you in my here and now is that they would have someone like the girl you knew with the cleft palate, the believer who gave up her life for Christ, and that her intercession would somehow communicate to people like you the love capable of conquering death. You, together with the women and men of today, need proof in the lives of others that the yoke of Jesus Christ really is sweet, and his burden light. The yoke is nothing more than the cross, the symbol of the unconditional love God has for all of his sons and daughters, even—no, especially—for those who want to believe.

Miss Havisham[1]

Dear Miss Havisham,

I consider you one of the most despicable characters ever to appear in a novel. Perhaps it is bad manners to begin a letter in such blunt fashion, but I find it suitable enough for you. For the record, I do not think that you are *the* most despicable literary person I have ever encountered—that distinction belongs to Cathy Bates, the villain of Steinbeck's classic *East of Eden.* You could, I suppose, derive some consolation from that.

Yes, despicable is the proper word, and unforgettably so. From the moment you lured young Pip into your insidious plot all the way to your equally wretched death, I had earmarked you as an enemy of charity and a fantastically miserable old woman. Yet such repulsive sentiments, however justified they might be, also made room for thoughts of pity as your story unfolded. I understand why you would feel like life itself stopped at twenty minutes to nine (as you set all your clocks permanently to that time) on the morning of your wedding day when your groom jilted you via a note.

Less comprehensible was your rooted determination to remain in that state of furious abandonment to such an extent that you closed yourself in your room, shut the curtains, daily wore your yellowed and faded wedding dress, and permitted the wedding cake to rot untouched over the sorrowful decades. Such sad eccentricities by themselves would be pardonable if they were limited to you. We all adopt irrational quirks in response to curious events, and no one can force anyone else to live beyond a fateful moment if they do not want to.

---

1. Miss Havisham is a character in the novel *Great Expectations* by Charles Dickens. Having been jilted by her fiancé on her wedding day, she later teaches a young girl to inflict the same kind of punishment on the main character, Pip, which had been inflicted on her.

But you gradually morphed into a monster of vengeance, and imposed your wrathful misery not on your wicked would-be groom, but on two innocent children. You fed your adopted Stella venomous plans to grip the heart of poor Pip, squeeze all possible happiness out of it, and then callously toss it to the ground. In short, you lived out an improvised commandment of your own devising: *Do unto others as has been done unto you.* You removed Stella's girlish heart and replaced it with ice, and once you grasped the gravity of your vicious deed in Pip's very presence, your frozen life met its end in fire. I will not dwell on Pip's warm and undeserved act of magnanimity that, perhaps, released you from that cold prison of yourself, mainly because I want my readers to read Mr. Dickens's masterpiece for themselves.

Miss Havisham, many who read the tale of your life will likely shudder at the possibility that such a creature as yourself could possibly be found on this earth. The sheer extravagance of your matrimonial mania seems absurd to normal, reasonable men and women. "That would *never* happen to me," they assure themselves after reading a description of your dismal room and your shrunken, skeletal body. Indeed, I would hope such a lifestyle as yours has not been replicated anywhere else other than in literature.

Yet I cannot but feel that you manifested in your literary flesh a spiritual malady of fearful *and all too common* proportions in the real world. Even as we lock away the indelible images and words of your madness, we likely fail to perceive the same diseased and destructive logic at work in our own thoughts: the effect of hot hatred over a slight or a terrible offense cooling over time into frozen vengeance, which ices our spiritual blood and destroys our own happiness, not to mention so many relationships with others.

Many centuries before you or I existed, Saint Bernard of Clairvaux diagnosed your condition, as well as that of many monks and laypeople he counseled. He defined it as a "hard heart," a phrase which is too mild for your case, but sufficiently conveys the dark reality of the disorder you inflicted on yourself:

> Now, what is a hard heart? One that is not torn by compunction, softened by piety, or moved by entreaty . . . It is ungrateful for kindness, treacherous in its advice, harsh in judgment, unashamed of disgrace, fearless in danger, inhuman toward humanity . . . This is a heart which recalls nothing at all from the past except injuries suffered, retains nothing of the present and makes neither provision nor preparation for the future, except perhaps in vengeance.[2]

2. Bernard of Clairvaux, *Five Books on Consideration*, 28.

You admitted as much to Pip when he confronted you with his dreadful state of soul. Saint Bernard certainly captures the essence of the hard heart's renunciation of charity and any human kindness, though I think the best image for such a spiritual state is that of *ice*—Dante deemed it the ideal surface for the lowest bowels of his *Inferno*, and Dante is usually right.

I mentioned, Miss Havisham, that I think this icing of the heart is terribly common in people who outwardly appear healthy and even happy. In response to a particular event of any sort—a betrayal, a failure, an unexpected shock of disappointment, wounded pride—anger lodges itself in the human heart, and kindles a white-hot fiery burning. Civility usually allows us to contain that irrational wrath in the immediate aftermath of our reaction, but that smoldering inferno cannot be sustained for long. Just as the prick of a bee sting soon yields to a heavy and swollen soreness of limb, so the fearsome red fury channels itself into a cold, calculating malice. The pulsing blood of love soon freezes, preventing any charitable thought for others from circulating, and the hurt caused by the offense becomes an all-consuming chilled wrath. The victim of the offense (for we love turning ourselves into victims) then broods and obsesses over the hurt, and connives ways to wreak vengeful havoc on the perpetrator.

You exemplified this poisoned process to devastating effect, but you imposed your icy will on someone besides yourself. Since you could not find happiness any longer, and had no means of avenging yourself on the man who spurned you on your wedding day, you turned your wrath on another representative of the male species, an innocent boy. In the hope of receiving some contemptible consolation to balm the wound you kept everfresh, you engineered that same experience of disgraceful wretchedness in poor Pip, who fell headfirst into your miserable trap.

I note this same cancer in many people who come to me for spiritual direction, Miss Havisham. They have allowed grudges against a friend or family member to harden into implacable hatred. Like you, they have discovered a cruel form of happiness by clinging to that past hurt and refusing to release it, thinking that they are somehow free in their enslavement to their icy fury. This thought process actually makes a sort of sense, for we instinctively comfort ourselves while wallowing in the misery of the past. Ice, after all, does not allow the warmth of love to draw near, and therefore we cannot be hurt again by some other knife-wound of betrayal or loss. The feeling of being cheated provides us with an excuse to nurse our wound without ever needing to deal with the arduous process of healing, which indeed can be terribly difficult. While we might not stop our clocks to recall the precise moment when our happiness ended, we do enclose ourselves in a cold shell of misery, from which we then channel our wrath in brooding silence, passive-aggressive comments or actions, and even violent outbursts.

The worst effect of this interior spiritual destruction, this movement from toxic fire to ice, is the self-loathing that is so obvious to someone outside of yourself. The total absence of charity from your heart, if we define charity as the desire for the good of another person, leads naturally to a loss of your own dignity. The heart, made to give and receive love, cannot accept the goodness of anyone else once you allow it to fixate exclusively on the laceration of the past. As a result, not only do you come to hate all of humankind, but you come to hate your very self, starved as you are of the love for which you were made.

Fortunately, an icy heart can be melted, but only with a determined and persistent effort of the will. The natural shock, anger, and even rage stemming from a betrayal or a tragic loss need not frost what should be a warm heart forever. You received an immense grace near the end of your life, Miss Havisham, from Pip himself, who refused to allow the same arctic malice to overcome him. Though sorely tempted to retain his bitter resentment at you and permit it to devour his heart as a spiritual cancer, he understood the need to live free of that cancer, unshackled from the icy chains of anger. And in setting himself free in your very presence, he turned a looking-glass on you that showed you what you had done to yourself. Note the compassion in the words of the boy you tried to pierce with your transplanted hate, but ultimately failed:

> I knew not how to answer, or how to comfort her. That she had done a grievous thing in taking an impressionable child to mould into the form that her wild resentment, spurned affection, and wounded pride, found vengeance in, I knew full well. But that, in shutting out the light of day, she had shut out infinitely more; that, in seclusion, she had secluded herself from a thousand natural and healing influences; that, her mind, brooding solitary, had grown diseased, as all minds do and must and will that reverse the appointed order of their Maker; I knew equally well. And could I look upon her without compassion, seeing her punishment in the ruin she was, in her profound unfitness for this earth on which she was placed, in the vanity of sorrow which had become a master mania, like the vanity of penitence, the vanity of remorse, the vanity of unworthiness, and other monstrous vanities that have been curses in this world?[3]

3. Dickens, *Great Expectations*, 394.

To your credit, you came to understand that ripping open the wound constantly, and then carving that same wound into the flesh of another person's soul, brought you only further misery. But your response to Pip's dramatic confession of compassion revealed the abyss of self-hatred into which you had cast yourself. Unaccustomed to charity, you could not accept charity or even forgiveness when it was offered to you. And that prevented you from forgiving yourself the harm you had done to Pip.

Your life can be a stern but very salutary warning to us, Miss Havisham. Life often presents us with choices between your reaction to the fiery anguish of hurt and Pip's. We are all wounded in innumerable ways by many people, and some of those knife-thrusts could congeal into frozen malice bent only on preserving the outrage and keeping us a victim to our own anger. I wish that your life would be a plea for forgiveness, for the urgency of healing from a wound of betrayal, lest the wound be replicated permanently in the soul. I would hope that the readers of your woeful tale would root out the identical wrath in their own hearts which led to your wretchedness, and that they would understand that a charitable future is only possible when the wicked security of a wrathful past is banished forever.

Alexander Graham Bell[1]

Dear Alexander Graham Bell,

Dear Alexander Graham Bell,

The brain is one of very few created things that no human being can claim to have invented. As curious as you and other inventors are, your automatic starting point for inquiry and discovery is the gift of your own grey matter. Among the many wonders of our noggins, memory has always fascinated me, particularly the mysterious manner in which some present phenomenon—be it a smell, song, or conversation with someone—can call to mind some fact or experience lodged in the far-distant past.

One such example occurred just this afternoon, and it directly concerns you. I was walking down the mall of the university campus where I teach, enjoying the egg-frying warmth of the Texas sun on my face. As I neared my building, a young woman brusquely pushed open the door with her forearm and shoulder and scooted into the sunshine. Her head was bowed, her hands folded and nearly touching, but she was not praying—she was engrossed with her cell phone wrapped in swaddling fingers and lying in her palm, perhaps texting a friend or scrolling through a website. She was totally oblivious to the world around her, which included me, strolling perhaps ten feet ahead of her and directly in her path. I stopped as she approached, aware that she was completely unaware of my presence. When she got within two paces or so, I dramatically jump-stepped to the side, certain that she would at that point be alerted that a near altercation was averted. But no, nothing about her surroundings registered at all, and she continued to stare at her phone as her feet autopiloted away from me.

You probably saw the word "phone" in my account of the collision-that-almost-was. An intelligent fellow like yourself could reasonably and

---

1. Alexander Graham Bell (1847–1922) was an inventor born in Scotland who settled in the United States. He is credited with the invention of the telephone.

correctly surmise that the phone in question is the descendant of the invention which earned you enduring fame: the telephone. The etymology of words is a topic of perpetual interest to me, and while still marveling at the narrowly avoided mash-up on the mall, I set to translating the Greek words you linked together to form that new English word. *Tēle*, meaning "far," or "from a distance," and related to the root meaning "end," "goal," or "purpose," is the first part, and *phōnē*, "voice," makes up the second. Combined, *telephone* makes clear the function of your wondrous contraption: a machine which relays a voice from a distance, from one end to the other!

Given your word choice for your great invention, I thought you would be eager to hear, via the "telephone" of writing, what your original idea has morphed into. I also feel a certain sense of duty to declare to you my feeling that the technology which you harnessed in the first telephone device is now being abused, to such an extent that it is destroying the very fabric of human relationships and humanity itself. That sounds quite grave, I admit. I shall explain myself.

Anyone walking down a busy city street will almost certainly be forced to sidestep a humanoid robot charging at him or her with a phone in the bayonet position. There are millions of automated hominids wandering the streets of America during the day, men and women who respond only to what their phones tell them to do at that particular moment (paper maps, by the way, are basically extinct). With video games, movies, music, social media, and endless apps now effortlessly available on portable eye-shackles we call phones, I worry that the diminishment of our humanity is proportionate to the rate at which technology makes itself necessary to aid us in being human. Subways and metro stations are naturally hostile to genuine human encounters, given the noise, grime, and shady characters who roam there. But with so many iPod-toting zombies zoning out the world with a glaze spread over their eyes, one cannot help but wonder whether the apocalypse is anticipated in this voluntary solitary confinement of apparently free people.

Parents often treat television as a babysitter for their children, and a dependency on images quickly takes root in the minds of impressionable toddlers and adolescents. Scores of adults, mature from a physical standpoint but entirely puerile in terms of moral conscience and life skills, have trapped themselves in a world governed by games and screens. The enormous waste of time devoted to such activities is distressing enough, and the morphing of normal human beings into bleary-eyed sleepwalkers with sore thumbs is hardly cause for joy. What concerns me more, however, is the sheer addictive behavior and accompanying dehumanization that has so quickly become the norm in regular society.

This phenomenon is not limited to specific hours of the day, certain locations whether public or private, or even a particular age group. I have witnessed a terrifyingly pathetic scene multiple times at restaurants: a family seated at the same table, a teenage boy with headphones plugging his ears and filling his brain with noise, a younger girl with her head bowed and thumbs finger-printing the screen of her phone, the father with an emotionless face casually scrolling, and the mother, twirling her forkful of pasta with forlorn eyes, tracing the contours of the painting on the wall across from her. I perceived that no one at the table sensed the need for direct interaction or eye contact with the other human beings around them, or even pondered that such a situation might be abnormal. What was once an occasion for gathering family and friends together, a meal, has become simply an extension of the rest of the day: one self absorbed in one's own virtual world while others do the same in theirs, a rather frightening case of being together and totally alone at the same time.

The fact that this occurs all the time now is the direct result of the revolution brought about by technology. The relentless news cycle flashes updates by the minute, offering text updates or email reminders acting as the bell did once to Pavlov's dog, provoking an instinctive expectation to be fed. The same goes for that insatiable human desire for entertainment. From sports highlights to petty celebrity gossip, from snapchats to tweets, from ongoing games with "friends" who have never met in real life to a glut of procrastination opportunities for college students with a paper due the next day—our phones have turned us into drones, Mr. Bell. We have become unfeeling monads incapable of deep thought or attentive reading beyond a quick headline and caption. A man recently wrote an article for *New York Magazine* on how he became manically addicted to the information bombardment of the omnipresent technology around him. The title of his article was "I Used to be a Human Being!"[2]

This monstrous craving for distraction, continuously sated only to create further hunger, is most lamentably evident in the explosion of pornography on the internet, a terrible scourge of humanity. This is sad proof that our lusts easily move us to degrade ourselves and our fellow human beings, viewed merely as flesh-pieces, to the level of beasts ruled by cruel passions.

2. Sullivan, "I Used to be a Human Being," paras. 1–7.

Does this shock you, Mr. Bell? Your original intention behind the telephone was, I believe, to connect voices so that distance would not be a barrier to communication. The purpose of communication, of course, is to strengthen bonds of love and communion, not to enslave individuals in addictive behaviors which isolate them from the very people they wish to communicate with. A wise man once said regarding television, "The medium is the message," and the message sent to us by the omnipotence of phones is that we must react with knee-jerk emotion to phenomena, lacking any processing time to meditate deeply on how we receive them and what they are doing to us socially and spiritually.

There are many possible paths to explore here, but I want to focus on the consequences of this rampant dependence on a totally phony world, one which I am convinced is sapping us of our very ability to be fully alive as human beings made for communion. As an educated man of the nineteenth century, you are surely acquainted with a philosophical fellow named Plato. He, or rather his character Socrates, foresaw the inevitable results produced by the addicting seduction of video games and moving images on a screen. He intuitively realized this several thousand years ago, long before cell phones acquired their ubiquitous dominance over human existence.

At a certain point in the famous dialogue *The Republic*, Socrates describes the perpetual state of ignorance in which most human beings unknowingly live.[3] Socrates paints for his listeners the verbal image of an underground cave in which people dwell. They have never emerged from the cave, and thus have never seen the sun. They do not move freely about the cave, for they are chained to a rocky wall and face a flat rock formation. Above and behind them is a perpetually burning fire, as well as other people holding various objects before the fire which throw shadows onto the wall facing the chained men and women. Unaware of both the fire and the shadow-making, the chained people consider those silhouettes to be real objects, for they do not know that the moving images in front of them are mere shades displayed at the will and whim of those projecting them. Their life is an unexamined one, their abode a cave of ignorance. Tragically, they do not reflect upon themselves or on the truth of the world. They have no acquaintance with, or desire for, the pursuit of wisdom or even community. In short, they do not know themselves, a most condemning phrase on the lips of Socrates.

3. Plato, *Republic*, Book 7.

Some people, though, manage to unshackle themselves and find a way upward to the mouth of the cave. At first, their eyes are blinded by the brilliance of the sun they have never encountered before. But if they emerge from their prison and remain outside the darkness long enough, their eyes will grow accustomed to the light. Then they will be able to see the objects themselves, rather than their shadows splashed upon the wall.

This analogy, Mr. Bell, represents the freedom of the philosopher, the seeker of wisdom who is not bound by the superficial images portrayed on the wall of the cave. The true philosopher is the one who successfully moves upward to the realm of "the forms," the really real ideas, having escaped from the enslaving world of what he or she thought was real in the cave.

Perhaps you can see why I regard twenty-first century society as a new embodiment of Plato's cave. What began in your brilliant mind as a wonderful means of enabling the living voice to remove boundaries of distance has devolved into a vast complex of games, movies, videos, social media, and images plastered on innumerable screens in the mad modern world. The telephone you conceived and patented conducted sound waves across a wire; today's masters of technology offer us shadows of moving objects. These images do not bear the impress of reality, but rather stamp us with shallow ideas that we mistake, out of ignorance, for the sum total of reality. They can so saturate the human brain that it simply becomes numb to the possibility of calm reflection and even social interaction of any sort beyond the merely superficial.

I do not blame you, Mr. Bell, as I report on the fruit of your genius. Communication among human beings, of course, is a perennial weakness and problem. Every individual and every generation must address and solve it according to their own lights and abilities. But that is precisely my worry with my generation and those that will come after me, who will know only a world of screens and rapid-fire messages. The phone today is a tool, neutral in itself, yet it is so powerful, so magnetic in its all-encompassing capabilities, that children are being taught unconsciously that the only source of truth are websites like Google and Wikipedia, and that normal human interaction must always be interfaced. We must save ourselves from the technology we created to help us.

Respectfully if pessimistically,

Fr. Thomas

P.S. - After reading through what I unloaded on you, I admit that my complaint about the phone is unjust and excessive. I must acknowledge the immense good that has come from your invention. It does in fact nurture the roots of our humanity, for our desire to share things pertinent to our lives is a fundamental good. Your phone makes that sharing possible in ways you perhaps envisioned but could not entirely foresee: the exchange of information, the fostering of a fascination with other parts of the world and cultures, the connection between lovers separated by distance, solutions to problems for individuals and governments. All of this has come about thanks to your desire to unite places and people across a wire. Ultimately, I am grateful to you, Mr. Bell, even though this letter was more of a rant than a reflection (sorry about that). I do regard the phone and all subsequent communication technology as a gift propelling people to the light; I simply don't want to see it drag us into a cave of isolation and illusion. Okay, now I'm really done!

Jerusalem[1]

To the Holy City, *Yerushalayim,*

Your name is daily on my lips and in my heart. Within a simple church whose white-tan limestone rock strikingly resembles the stones of your Western Wall, my brother monks and I chant the same prayers as pilgrims lining your streets did more than 2,500 years ago. The prayer book of those faithful Israelites ascending the steps of the Temple mount, a collection of hymns uttered by Jesus himself, is the book of Psalms, and it forms the foundation of our prayer.

Within these sacred pages is a compendium of every human emotion under the sun, directed always toward the Lord who created us, chose Israel to be a people set apart, and selected you to be the place where his name would dwell (Deut 12:11). Joyful shouts of praise, anguished laments, songs of thanksgiving both individual and collective, pleas for help, cries of vengeance, a review of the Lord's saving action in the life of Israel—these words still rise daily like incense to the God of Abraham, Isaac, and Jacob from every corner of the earth.

You, so the Psalmist sings, are the city belonging to the Lord, the God of Israel; you are the mother of future generations, even future nations (Ps 87). The summit on which you are situated, Mount Zion, is "a superb elevation, the joy of all the earth"—not just the capital of King David's realm, but the very center of the world (Ps 48). The Lord selected you to house his dwelling place, the Ark of the Covenant, within the Temple sanctuary (Ps 135:21). Your location itself, a defensive stronghold surrounded by mountains, testifies to the Lord's watchful and loving protection of you (Ps 125). Psalms 120–134, each of which begins with the phrase "a psalm of ascents"

---

1. Jerusalem is "the holy city," the capital of David's kingdom and the site of Jesus' crucifixion.

or "a psalm of the steps," were perhaps composed for pilgrims approaching your gates and then the sanctuary itself to offer their sacrifices to the Lord. That series concludes with the beautiful petition, "May the Lord bless you from Zion, he who made heaven and earth" (Ps 134:3).

For as long as I can remember, I greatly desired to set foot in the land of my ancestors in faith, to be a pilgrim like so many millions before me, and to tread in the very places where Jesus, my Christ, taught and prayed and died and rose again. Both the Old and New Testaments note that every traveler ascends or goes up to reach you, and those who depart always go down from your heights, regardless of the direction they take. I wanted, like the inspired poet who penned Psalm 102, to love your very stones, to be moved with pity even at the sight of your dust. I wished patiently for many years to experience firsthand the truth expressed in Psalm 50:2: "Out of Zion, the perfection of beauty, God shines forth."

One of the great privileges of my life was the opportunity to spend a month within your gates (Ps 122), to walk upon and count the ramparts of your old city wall (Ps 48), to kneel down and kiss your ground, and to say "Hallelujah" where that prayer, which literally means "Praise the Lord," was first formulated and chanted. My school in Rome, the Pontifical Biblical Institute (or Biblicum for short), requires every student to take a course in "the geography and archaeology of the Holy Land." Students have the option of learning about the characters, contours, and sites of the Bible either in a stuffy Roman classroom or at the places themselves. Few decisions have ever been so easy for me to make, and I was extremely grateful that my abbot permitted me to take the on-site course.

My classmates and I, assembling from about twenty countries, were no ordinary pilgrims. We came principally to read the pages of "the fifth Gospel," a fitting summary for the land of Israel. Our teachers and guides were two Franciscan friars who had lived there for more than thirty years, and had participated in excavations at Christian sites such as Capernaum, Nazareth, and Bethlehem. Their expertise and evident love of the land were gifts they willingly shared with us wherever we stopped. Our travels took us "from Dan to Beer-Sheba" (Judg 20:1), by tradition the northernmost and southernmost borders of biblical Israel.

These intensive weeks in Israel were a biblical student's dream: a continuous bathing in the waters of history, archaeology, and Scripture. From a spiritual perspective, I found many "thin places" which nourished my soul. A "thin place" could be any site at which the barrier between heaven and earth, between the individual and God, seems to become transparent, or at least permeable. It is personal holy ground, a space where God is somehow more immediate, more present, than anywhere else. The thinnest place I discovered in the land was Capernaum, the headquarters for Jesus' initial ministry in Galilee, right on the tranquil Sea of Galilee (Matt 9:1). Nothing makes reading the Bible fresher and more fascinating than the ability to recall my own memories of the names and places I find in the sacred pages.

But our headquarters were in your midst, Jerusalem, and my most indelible experiences took place within your walls. Before arriving, I was aware that you were and are the precious jewel claimed by Jews, Christians, and Muslims. What I discovered during my brief visit there was indeed the holy city, but also the city of human nature—a place of stunning beauty and tragic anger, a tapestry of glory and misery woven of gold thread and garbage, the site of surprising tolerance and intolerable reminders of racial hatred and religious division.

Our Franciscan professors guided us through the various stages of your growth, evidenced by the ancient city walls buried beneath the modern city. We traversed the Roman streets (the intersecting *cardo* and *decumanus*, so uniform across the cities of the empire), and we walked around the most recent of walls fortifying what is now the old city, dating to the time of Suleiman the Magnificent in the seventeenth century. Within Suleiman's walls today, but outside the city walls at the time of Jesus' crucifixion, is Mount Calvary, enclosed by the Church of the Holy Sepulchre. At the most sacred place in all of Christendom, both the site of the crucifixion and the stone tomb in which Jesus was laid, one would expect to find a peaceful and dignified area worthy of the tremendous memory it preserves. Instead, I found the saddest evidence of the divisions which continue to rend the Body of Christ. The church itself is divided into sections, guarded and operated by different ecclesial groups: the Armenian Orthodox, the Greek Orthodox, the Roman Catholic Franciscans, etc. Each claims a piece of the hallowed turf, and willingly resorts to violence if someone encroaches on their parcel. The church, depressingly dark, is in shambles because the factions cannot agree on desperately needed renovations (though thankfully, I hear that some work is underway right now).

I returned to the Mount of Olives multiple times, both with classmates and by myself. I had only thought of the place as the site of Jesus' agony in the garden, so I was stunned to find the majority of the vast hill covered with white tombs. I recall opening my prayer book to Zechariah 14, and reading a prophecy that the Lord will return to you from the east, coming from the Mount of Olives to establish his eschatological reign. According to Jewish tradition, the dead lying here in wait will be restored to life when the Messiah comes to the holy city. The view of your city from this vantage point is simply breathtaking.

The building that dominates the vista, of course, is the gleaming golden Dome of the Rock. My fascination with the layers of history was most evident when my professors discussed this particular place. I marvel at the continuity of mankind, in this instance at how one specific spot can be such a thin place for generations of peoples of different religions and races. This area, perhaps originally a Canaanite sanctuary, was home to the First and Second Temples, then a Roman temple dedicated to Jupiter, then a Christian site, and is presently a Muslim mosque. It has, of course, been a source of constant strife as Jews, Christians, and Muslims have fought to regain it. Beneath the Dome of the Rock is the Western Wall, the last remaining portion of the Second Temple precincts and the most venerable site for the Jewish people. Rather than put a written petition in one of the crevices, I simply wanted to stand and pray alongside the faithful Jews who were reading from their books, rocking back and forth in prayerful rhythm and touching the wall with unspeakable longing in their eyes for the restoration of that ruined Temple.

What struck me at every site associated with the life of Jesus was the indescribable fact that my Lord and Messiah himself set foot here—not in my present here and now, to be sure, but the barriers of time and space were nevertheless powerless to prevent my awareness of his presence. His footprints, though not visible today on your stones or in your dust, brought my feet to your streets, and in a way perhaps only a believer can grasp (that is, with the logic of the heart), the same "here," in this place, united myself and my Lord in a most lovely way. The perception that the love of God was present in Christ 2,000 years ago and equally present within me *in the exact same place* is the greatest gift I received. I was astounded at my meditation that the very love which our God *is*, and which emptied himself into the person Jesus Christ, desired me to see with my own eyes what Jesus saw with his.

When the time came for us to depart, an inevitable sadness took root in my heart. I left with the sincere hope of returning once more, but the sadness was not simply a product of the journey's end. One way of saying goodbye in modern Hebrew is *Shalom, habar*, literally, "Peace, friend," and

I pondered the meaning of the word "peace." Even now, Jerusalem, I admit that I am perplexed when I read the instruction in Psalm 122 to "Pray for the peace of Jerusalem." I confess that I do not know what to pray for, or how that peace, whatever its definition, might come about.

Your very name, *Yerushalayim*, contains the root letters of *shalom*. I suppose that Jews, Christians, and Muslims will understand the peace of Jerusalem in different ways. The authors of the New Testament books, from Matthew to John to Paul, understood that the Jewish Scriptures had to be read in the light of Jesus of Nazareth's claim to be the Messiah, the anointed one, the savior of Israel. Matthew applies to Jesus the words of Micah 5:4, "He shall be peace," words which seemed to foretell the coming of a peaceful reign. This reign of peace, inaugurated by the Messiah, was conceived by Isaiah as a paradise, where animals and humans would exist in harmony and the ruler of Israel would be a righteous descendant of David. In another passage, Isaiah foresaw a future time in which many nations would come to you and say, "'Come, let us go up to the mountain of the Lord, to the house of the God of Jacob, that He may instruct us in His ways, and that we may walk in His paths.' For from Zion shall go forth *Torah*, and the word of the Lord from Jerusalem" (Isa 2:3).

Yet while Christians believe that Jesus was the promised descendant of David and the Messiah, he certainly did not bring about a peaceful reign within your walls as the prophets envisioned—the Romans destroyed you and the Temple in AD 70, and utterly demolished you again in AD 135. Jeremiah's words continue to stand today as a sign of lament and incompleteness: "Peace, peace, they say—but there is no peace" (Jer 6:14).

I think the absence of earthly peace naturally led the New Testament writers to assert that you, the earthly city, would yield to a new Jerusalem, a heavenly city. Evidence for this movement from earthly to heavenly is abundant, especially in Philippians 3:19 and Hebrews 11, but its most dramatic presentation comes in the book of Revelation, the magnificent concluding book of the New Testament, where the new and definitive Jerusalem is presented as descending from the sky to meet her groom, Christ the Lamb (Rev 19–22). The peace "which the world cannot give" (John 14:27) thus necessitated that Christians not look to you as the summit of their eternal hopes, but rather to a celestial city which eye has not yet seen.

How, then, should I pray for peace within your walls? The current situation and the wickedness of division so prevalent in human relations suggest that any temporal peace, however longed for in prayer, is impossible to achieve. This does not mean that we should give up hope of reconciliation among brothers and sisters in the land of Israel, but it does leave a constant sorrow in my heart for the victims of violence in that land. Yet both forms of faith are difficult to accept. The reality of hatred, festering over generations and leading frequently to injustices and war, renders any peace accomplished by men subject to failure. The Christian longing for a future Jerusalem, on the other hand, can give the appearance of abandoning the present mess for a pie in the sky hope detached from reality.

Near the end of his life, Jesus lamented that your inhabitants rejected him. He spoke of himself as a mother hen wishing to gather her young under her wing, "but you were unwilling" (Matt 23:37). But he also spoke, after predicting that "your house will be abandoned," of a time when you will say, "Blessed is he who comes in the name of the Lord" (Luke 13:34–35; also Matt 23:37–39; Luke 19:41–44). That confession cannot and will not be coerced, but I simply don't know when and how it would come about.

There is a beautiful phrase in 2 Peter 3:8, drawn directly from Psalm 90:4, that "with the Lord one day is as a thousand years and a thousand years are as one day." The author then proceeds to describe how the heavens as we know them will pass away, and he speaks of this occurrence as "the day of the Lord," a phrase often on the mouths of the prophets. Revelation foretells of "a new heaven and a new earth," but it does not state that our world will be wiped out and destroyed forever. Why? Because what descends from the new heaven is "the holy city, Jerusalem," presented as a bride adorned to meet her beloved (Rev 21:1–2, 10). This definitive conclusion of temporal history cannot be absolute; if it were, your name would not be associated with the heavenly city we await at the end of time.

There must, in other words, be some continuity between the earthly city and the heavenly one. There must exist, somehow, a real identity between what you are now on earth and what the holy city will be at "the wedding feast of the Lamb" (Rev 19:6–10). Just as the bodies of Jesus (and, as Catholics believe, Mary) are both different than and yet identical with their earthly bodies, so too we can hope that you, Jerusalem, will be transformed and spiritualized, preserved somehow for that final victory of God.

We are assured that all that is holy and precious in this world will be taken up in the world to come. This understanding of the end, therefore, does not at all absolve us of our duty to promote peace within your borders now. It rather demands it, even as it consoles us that what we love in you will be preserved, as God best determines it, in the eternal and timeless day of the Lord.

Perhaps this reflection on peace helps me formulate what I experienced within your sacred walls. The here of Jesus became my here for a short period of time in the movement from past to present, united by place. The same movement, though on an unimaginably grander and more transcendent scale, will take place from present to future, meaning that my experience of the love of God while in your midst is simply a foretaste, a faint image, of the eternal glory to be revealed in the fullness of time.

That is my sincere hope, Jerusalem. I do not know when or how the nations will come streaming toward your gates. I pray that the people within your gates at present will never cease to call upon the name of the Lord, to be a blessing to everyone in their midst, and seek to walk humbly with their God. I can promise you that I will pray that peace, the absence of war, and brotherhood among peoples, be realized within your walls, and that I may contemplate all of God's children assembled together in the heavenly city when our earthly sojourn is completed. I will also, selfishly but sincerely, pray that I might be blessed to count your earthly ramparts one more time before I die.

The Angelus Peasants[1]

To *The Angelus* peasants,

I apologize for my lack of formality in greeting you. Much like the sinful woman of Luke 7, your names are unknown to me. In spite of my ignorance of your proper names, I hope you will happily accept this surprise letter from a total (but friendly!) stranger.

My acquaintance with you is due entirely to a painting which fascinated me upon my first viewing of it, and is still projected frequently onto the screen of my mind. I do not know whether Mr. Jean-François Millet asked you to pose for the painting, or if he simply observed you harvesting potatoes in a field somewhere in France and then did the imaginative work in his head. Whatever the case may be, *The Angelus* quickly became one of the most recognizable canvases in Europe, and it continues to be a favorite attraction at the prestigious Musée d'Orsay in Paris. In the event that you haven't seen it, I will describe it to you. Given that I do not know your names, I will simply refer to "the man" and "the woman" in the third person, just as I would if I were speaking about this painting to a group of students who do not have the image before their eyes.

Dusk is settling on an open field as the sun sets outside the canvas to the left. Clouds smeared a dull dark grey, partnering with a scattered flock of black birds, are slowly gathering at the top and right. Some streaks of pink, pale blue, and green seem to form an arc from the sunward side, perhaps attempting to push the clouds back and stall the inevitable onset of evening.

Two figures are set squarely in the foreground of the picture: a man stands center-left, a woman center-right. Farmland occupies most of the

1. *The Angelus* is a painting by Jean-François Millet (1814–1875) displayed in the Musée d'Orsay in Paris. It features two farmers, a man and a woman, praying in an open field as the afternoon sun sets.

canvas, and creates the horizon line with the sky at the shoulders of the woman. Rows of weed-like potato plants are visible behind the man. The land beneath their feet is rough—browns and dark greens, mottled and splotchy, unpolished smudges resemble ragged leaves and the toughness of turf, all form the terrain, at once rugged and flat. Behind the primary patch of ground, a slightly more verdant field lures the eye back toward the horizon line, with small rocks or shrubs interspersed in no apparent order. In the distance to the right, a church steeple stands tall, accompanied by a smattering of tiny tree clusters to the right.

My attention rightly focuses on the couple, probably a husband and wife, at their humble and lifelong farming trade. Mr. Millet has captured them in what I would call a human still-life pose as they pause from their labors. The man has fixed his three-pronged pitchfork in the soil to his right, leaving its handle pointing skyward but at a slightly tilted angle. The woman apparently just let go of her wheelbarrow, placed behind her in the painting. The man is wearing a white shirt covered by a plain brown jacket, blue pants, and round clogs for shoes. The woman sports a long work apron, white but dirtied by peasant duties, and wrapped around her left forearm is a pink sleeve. A white bonnet crowns her head and covers her hair, and brown rags seem to be draped around her feet.

Ah, the pure simplicity and beauty of their postures! The sun creeping toward the horizon produces shadows on their faces, which prevent any clear features from being detected. The man solemnly bends his head, his body still erect with the pride of an honest peasant, but his shoulders stoop, laden with the invisible weight generated by decades of tough farming. He holds a dark cap gently in his hands; his thumbs are the only visible digits. The woman's head is likewise bowed, but she seems to incline downward more so than the man, and her whole body follows that inclination. Her hands are clasped piously to her chest. Both of them fix their gaze on the earth they have just been tilling, inattentive to their darkening surroundings.

The title of Millet's painting suggests the motive for the prayerful pause at the end of a hard day's labor. The *Angelus*, a meditation on the biblical scene in which the angel Gabriel announces to Mary that she will conceive and bear a son named Jesus, is still recited today by Catholics of all ages and nationalities. The simple prayer, composed of the biblical verses themselves and a series of Hail Marys, reminds those praying of the new life for all that is made possible by Christ, and allows them to recall the great dignity afforded to Mary, all mothers, and indeed all the faithful who bear the name of Christian. The *Angelus* corresponds beautifully to the grace suffusing the simple peasant life: the prayer generates the recognition of one's humble estate in life, whether one is a farmer, a doctor, or even a priest, and reaffirms one's dependence on God for all things physical as well as spiritual.

But a final detail in the painting whose meaning eludes me has prompted me to write to you. At the feet of both the man and the woman is a small wicker basket. Lying within the basket are perhaps a dozen potatoes, newly picked from the field. Now, a potato basket by itself is not such a significant element; one would expect to find such an object on a canvas featuring two farmers picking the fruit of the earth. What greatly intrigues me about the basket, rather, is the combination of its shape and the postures of the couple surrounding it. The way in which the eyes of both the man and the woman fall upon it, as well as the somber presentation of their bodies, suggests something much more dramatic to my mind. I have the impression, however unfounded it may be, that the couple is mourning a child, and that the basket strongly resembles a tiny coffin soon to be interred in the earth.

I am not the only viewer who perceives a funerary arrangement here. A famous twentieth-century painter, Salvador Dalí, used this painting frequently as inspiration for his own creativity. Frankly, he offered many weird interpretations of the painting. I bring him up here only because he reportedly asked a museum to x-ray the canvas, convinced that Millet originally painted a coffin and then replaced it with a potato basket. The results supposedly confirmed Dalí's hypothesis, but I have not found specific confirmation of this. Not everyone agrees with this assessment of the scene. One of my confreres is of the opinion that the woman is too calm to be burying a child; he also notes the odd choice of a potato field as the location for a burial!

We will likely never know how the artist produced his painting. I would love to know if Mr. Millet gave you any hint about his intention for this masterpiece. Was he paying homage to a way of life soon to be threatened by industrial advancement, which would soon rip human beings from their rustic connection to the earth, replacing that immediate link with a world of cold concrete, steel, and glass? Did he simply wish to acknowledge his own nostalgia for the religious belief of the simple peasant? Did he desire to share an insight regarding the condition of humanity as tied to the earth and, for that reason, destined for a mortal harvest?

Whenever I look at the painting, I think of the essential connection we human beings have to the earth. This natural affinity goes beyond the biblical assertion in Genesis 2:7 that the human being is created from the dust of the earth, a timeless truth confirmed by modern biology and chemistry. I find the link most perfectly communicated in the knowledge of how our precious and precarious life, often as uncertain as a harvest, is ever tending toward death, as certain as the setting sun. This inexorable fact of our mortality often surprises, angers, and drives us to tremendous depths of despair if we ignore death, or think of it only as something desperately to be avoided.

One particular experience will help me to frame just what I mean. During my studies in Rome, my parents flew over to pay me a visit. Since military service runs deep in both their families, I wanted to take them to the small town of Nettuno, home to a World War II cemetery containing the graves of American soldiers who lost their lives during the Battle of Anzio and the subsequent Italian Campaign in 1944. At the cemetery, a simple fountain and pool greeted us, behind which lay a giant field of recently mowed grass. To the left and right of this central area were the graves of over 7,800 Americans. The tombstones are made of white marble. Almost all of them took the form of a simple cross (though there were also occasional Stars of David). They were arranged in rows of long and gently sweeping arcs; the gradual curvature of the rows reminded me of the seating design for an amphitheater. We were not allowed to walk among the graves, so we stayed on the main path, lined with tall Roman pine trees. At a certain angle, the crosses in one row would merge together, creating the optical effect of a single curved line of crosses. A movement forward would then reveal the individual headstones, each now standing unique within its row.

My parents and I took a train back to Rome after spending some sober minutes on the nearby Anzio shore, where the Allied soldiers landed on their way to the capital city. The course of the regional train brought to view from the window many fields of vines and stakes. The train moved so quickly that I could see the stakes merging into a single line and then diverging just as quickly. My eyes beheld the unifying of vines ever so briefly as single columns and then their separating just as rapidly, in a span of seconds, into isolated stakes. The same pattern formed before my eyes as that in the amphitheater-like rows of graves. In that singular experience, the shared geometry of graveyard and vineyard yielded a common insight between human life and the fruits of the earth in my mind: the cycle of life and death is imposed on each human being, just as it is on the world of plants and dust.

Sir and madam, I am living in an age in which many people no longer even set foot on real earth at any point in their day. A friend recently shared with me her joy at the rare opportunity to put a shovel into the ground and plant vegetables on a weekend away from work. She noted that the dirt in her fingernails and a few scratches on her arms reminded her of the humanity she feels draining out of her while she sits in a fluorescent-lit office cubicle, whiling away the hours listening to "white noise" and staring at a computer screen. She experienced the simple truth manifest in the painting depicting the two of you in the potato field: those who *feel* the earth between their fingers know that they too are part of the mortal cycle returning all things to dust. Yet my friend knows, as you did, that the promise of new life springs necessarily from the apparent deadness of the land in winter.

And this thought leads me back to the *Angelus* prayer itself. The faith of the peasant, the simple life which you experienced together as man and woman, is far more real than any artificial city-dwelling on the part of enlightened folk. What they shield themselves from, in fact, is precisely what is so naturally plain to you: the earth, with its plantings and harvests, can awaken in us the awareness that our Creator intends joys and sorrows for us now, birth and death together, but also the certainty of a final sunrise after a dark night, *now and at the hour of our death. Amen.*

Abbot Wendelin Endrédy, O.Cist.[1]

To the Very Reverend Wendelin Endrédy, abbot of the Cistercian Abbey of Zirc:

This letter comes to you from a spiritual son whom you never met, living in a country far from your native land. I am a member of the Cistercian Abbey of Our Lady of Dallas, originally a small branch forcibly cut from the tree of Zirc, its motherhouse, but now grown into a blossoming tree, whose young roots have been continuously nourished by your prayers. Although I was born the year after your birthday into eternal life, I consider my Cistercian vocation to be the fruit of your saintly courage and patient endurance in this mortal valley of tears.

A few Cistercians who fled Hungary during the Communist persecution in the forties and fifties are still alive, and at present they form the elderly generation of my monastic community. As you know, some of them went into exile before the Abbey of Zirc was suppressed in 1950 and before you were arrested. Several others never had the chance to live as monks in the motherhouse of Zirc itself, but received their formation in an underground novitiate directed by Fr. Lawrence Sigmond during your years in prison.

Those Hungarian Cistercians still alive in the monastery I call home retain vivid memories of you, whether from their own interactions with you or from eyewitnesses to your immense suffering. They have shared willingly with the young American monks a sobering but inspiring portrait

---

1. Wendelin Endrédy (1898–1981) was the abbot of the Cistercian Abbey of Zirc in Hungary when the Communist regime suppressed it in 1950. While in prison, he was tortured and subjected to repeated humiliations. After being freed during the short-lived 1956 Hungarian Revolution, he was arrested again, and spent the remaining years of his life under house arrest at the Benedictine Abbey of Pannonhalma. The Cistercian Abbey of Our Lady of Dallas, the home of the author of these letters, is a "daughter house" of the Abbey of Zirc.

of you during a terrifyingly harsh time for the Christian faith and Hungarian people. Their stories, not to mention the Cistercian life they brought to Texas from Hungary, have rooted me and my American confreres in a tradition both humbled (by persecution) and humbling (on account of its eventual triumph over evil). Yours is a story I wish more people were acquainted with, especially given the shocking ignorance of history even of events experienced by those still living.

During my novice year and the years I spent in formation as a junior brother, my confreres and I received *puncta* (conferences) about your life. For spiritual reading, we were given pastoral letters you wrote to your monks, already scattered not only in Hungary but also outside its borders, as the Communist menace grew more and more threatening in the late 1940s. While I understood that you could not criticize the regime in such a public forum, I marveled at your assessment of the deteriorating situation as you exhorted your monks to greater holiness and love for each other. Given the imminent nationalization of the Cistercian schools and the increasing threat of suppression, the urgent force of your words in one particular paragraph from your 1947 letter is as startling as it is inspiring. You write to your Cistercian sons:

> The people expect the Spirit of Christ from us and, should they be disappointed, they may perhaps lose Christ again for centuries. We ought to prove ourselves before them as true men, teachers and educators according to the Spirit of Christ. We ought to be true priests of Christ, and monks who will follow Christ in everything. We ought to bear witness to the Spirit of Christ with our every act, with our whole life, because otherwise this generation, a "generation of those seeking God," will damn itself.[2]

At the beginning of your February 1949 letter, you clearly foresee the coming demise of Zirc and your own arrest, yet you firmly fix the eyes of your Cistercian sons on Christ, whose sufferings yielded to ultimate glory:

> The earnest words of the Savior have again interrupted the carnival's cacophony: "Behold, we are going up to Jerusalem, and everything written by the prophets about the Son of Man will be fulfilled. He will be handed over into the hands of the Gentiles; he will be mocked and spat upon, and after they have scourged him, they will kill him—but on the third day he will rise" (Luke 18:31–34).

2. My confrere, Fr. Roch Kereszty, translated all of the passages I quote from abbot Wendelin's unpublished pastoral letters to his monks.

I love the opening line, in which you subtly mock the powers of darkness encroaching upon your life. How could a young novice like myself not be invigorated by the fearless grace so manifest in those words? I could hear the echo of a prophetic voice from the Old Testament, isolated by the enemies of faith but fiercely loyal to the Lord's call, in your interpretation of the ominous gloom engulfing your country:

> We should strive all the more to promote with love and prayer the salvation of our fellow men and women, because we must partly make up for our own negligence. Of those who are stumbling around today in darkness, some may have gone astray because at one time in the past our light did not shine in such a way that they could have recognized in us our Father, who is in Heaven (Matt 5:16). Only God knows how much penance we still have to do for those who have gone astray because of us.

Abbot Wendelin, some people might resent what they perceive to be an absolution of the communist criminals in your words. What I read in them is your own confession of the sins committed by other people as well as your own, a bearing of the guilty burden which others cannot carry. I can only marvel at the spiritual courage you injected into your monks; these words must have been emboldening blood coursing into their frightened hearts at a time when ominous threats would soon yield to real persecution.

You entered into your own agony soon after that letter was written, much like the Lord whom you so lovingly served, yet your constant concern was for your brothers. Your devotion to them was already evident in your decision to return to Hungary in 1948 after meeting with the Holy Father in Rome. You knew that you were returning to certain peril, yet you, the captain, did not abandon the ship even though you could not control the winds or the waters.

Several confreres who have since passed away told of your foresight in sending monks to America before the puppet government loyal to Stalin could arrest them. Their task was to scope out a place where they could transplant their Cistercian life of monasticism, priestly ministry, and education of the young. You surely had no inkling that most of them would settle in Texas; you simply trusted that the winds of apparently random fortune would blow them where the Holy Spirit willed. Many of the brothers who eventually arrived in America took part in a dramatic escape across the Hungarian border into Austria in September 1950, though of the twenty-one who started out, only thirteen successfully avoided arrest and made their way to freedom. We have been fortunate to record the accounts of many of those brave escapees before they passed away.

Just weeks before you were ordered to hand the monastery of Zirc over to the communists, a boy of fourteen with aspirations to be a Cistercian joined you and a small group of monks for evening prayer. He had previously served Mass for you during one of your pastoral visits to the Cistercian school and parish in Székesfehérvár. I know that young man as Fr. Denis Farkasfalvy, abbot of the Dallas Abbey when I entered and under whose guidance I became a Cistercian. He recently shared his experience of that evening in October 1950 at my prompting. Knowing the abbey would soon be suppressed, he was received into the Order as an oblate, and would, several years later, be a clandestine novice under the protection of Fr. Lawrence.

Fr. Denis translated your memoirs into English in 1998, publishing them in a volume called *Cistercians in Texas* on the nine-hundredth anniversary of the establishment of the Cistercian Order. He, as well as the other Hungarians in Texas, clearly understood that our roots were strengthened by your tears and anguish in the years following the suppression of Cistercian life in Hungary. Your memoirs provide us with your own gruesome account of the savage sufferings you endured during six years of agony: your arrest on totally false charges of espionage and conspiracy with foreign governments, your show trial, the tortures you endured at the hands of godless officers, and the horrid details of your solitary confinement.

You may be surprised to know that I have set foot in one of the terrible buildings where you endured torments. The building located at 60 Andrássy Street, one of the busiest streets in downtown Budapest, had been the headquarters of the "Arrow Cross," the Hungarian Nazi party, during their short reign over Hungary in 1944 and 1945. When the Soviets expelled them near the end of World War II, the chief of the hated AVO, the Hungarian secret police, immediately set up shop there, and turned it into a multi-level horror show featuring interrogations, tortures, sham trials, solitary confinement cells, and executions of "enemies of the state." I am told that you were tortured there, and that a mockery of a trial was conducted within those wretched walls.

After the fall of communism in 1989 (which you sadly did not live to see), the building was converted into a museum, and is now aptly named the "House of Terror." The lobby area is dominated by a Soviet tank, with oil slowly dripping down the pedestal on which it stands. Overlooking the tank are two walls of photographs, revealing the victims of Communist inhumanity, many of whom were probably detained or even executed in that very building. The museum route takes visitors through rooms featuring films chronicling the spread of the Iron Curtain after World War II, Moscow propaganda in the form of advertisements and posters exhorting the workers to love "their" party and government, artifacts such as Khrushchev's automobile, and video testimonials from victims who were not silenced. In addition to explanations about the policies of the puppet regime in Hungary, which included the exploitation of farmers and the arrest of political and religious dissidents (such as your friend, Cardinal József Mindszenty), the various rooms also feature quotations on the walls from survivors who witnessed unspeakable atrocities.

Your name is prominently displayed in several places. I will never forget descending to the lowest level in an elevator and making my way to the solitary cells, where you and many other prisoners were kept. The quotation near the door leading to the corridor of cells was taken from your memoirs; you recalled praying to God that He would obliterate your memory before an interrogation session, so that you would not divulge any names or useful information to your torturers. The thought of you suffering in any one of the various chambers I walked through, all of them bereft of natural light and surely frigid in winter, with the knowledge that the next round of cruelty could very well kill you, haunted me. I was numbed by your account of the savage tortures you endured: the mind-altering chemicals injected into you in the hope of extracting a confession from you during interrogations were only the beginning of the psychological and physical abuse so senselessly inflicted upon you. Even when you were not being physically traumatized by police officers, you did not know a moment's peace: you wrote of the 700 some bedbugs you killed over a two-day period, of your inability to lie down on the bed, of the sewage which dripped on you from overhead pipes, and of the soldiers who blew their cigarette smoke at you and yelled obnoxiously whenever you managed to get bread and wine to celebrate Mass.

You were spared death, though you must have seen your fellow citizens walking down the corridor to the scaffold at the end of the hall. Beyond their ability to slaughter dissidents, the communists in Hungary were even more masterful at smashing the souls of individuals, who emerged from those years forever scarred by their experiences of intimidation, humiliation, and corporal pain. A dear confrere of mine, Fr. Pascal Kis-Horvath, was a relative of yours. He endured nightmares about his tortures during his four-year prison term for the rest of his life. Behind his sweet smile and playful demeanor, he was a broken man with a shattered psyche. Yet his fidelity to his Cistercian vocation was nothing short of heroic. On the date when his temporary vows as a monk expired, he was behind bars, unable to renew them in your presence. Undeterred, he renewed his profession by writing out his vows—in his own blood. Father Lawrence is another hero to my Hungarian confreres in Dallas. He became the leader of the Zirc monks after your arrest and was later incarcerated, but when the police realized that his kidney cancer was fatal (helped, no doubt, by the beatings he received in jail), they released him so that he would not be hailed as a martyr for dying in police custody.

The most vivid memory of my time in the House of Terror remains, strangely enough, my exit from the building and emergence onto the present-day street. I was greeted by perfume ads and peppy sports drink peddlers taking up the sidewalk space. I cannot describe how jarring the contrast from interior to exterior was. How unreal it all seemed, to walk out of a dungeon of death, where the walls themselves bear witness to the fearsome barbarism of the communist police, a place where untold numbers of innocent Hungarians perished (whether in body or soul)—and then to receive the glowing rays of the warm sun on my face! It was as though nature itself was forcefully encouraging me to dismiss the horror I had just experienced as a relic of the unpleasant past.

I know that you mercifully experienced an exit from that hell during the brief revolution of October 1956. You were freed from prison, only to be rearrested when the rebellion was put down by Soviet reinforcements. Yet you were eventually allowed to "retire" to house arrest at the Benedictine Abbey of Pannonhalma. By all accounts, you seem to have kept your sanity, and did not succumb to the vile attempts to destroy your faith or your mental health. I don't know if I would have the psychological strength to withstand such pressure for so long.

I do not need to share the initial years of Cistercian life in Irving, Texas with you, because I know you were well informed about the monks and their plans. Just recently, Fr. Denis began to translate a huge cache of letters exchanged between you and Fr. Anselm, the first abbot of my community. You seemed to correspond with Abbot Anselm every other week, and those letters promise to reveal fascinating glimpses of my community's founding and difficult first years. I also know that you were allowed to see visitors at Pannonhalma, even though the conversation always had to be guarded since the room was bugged. Father Roch Kereszty, my novice master, told me that he visited you in 1972, when travel to Hungary was permitted to foreigners. He came with two students from our Cistercian Preparatory School in Dallas; he said that you recognized both of them because you had seen their photos in the school yearbook, and you knew that they both had younger brothers in the school. One of those students was Peter Verhalen; he is presently my abbot, indeed the first American abbot of Our Lady of Dallas!

I do not quite know why I set out to write you this letter, Abbot Wendelin. I often experience a strange inner compulsion to write, and in this present case I feel as though I have been gently pressured by grace to thank you for your witness to our Christian faith and Cistercian vocation. While my gratitude counts for very little, and amounts to nothing at all when compared with the unapproachable light in which the Lord has called you to dwell for endless ages, it is perhaps for my own sake that I tell you that your unimaginable suffering during your earthly years was not in vain. After the collapse of Communism in 1989, your beloved Zirc was restored, and the monks of Dallas consider the well-being of our motherhouse to be vital to our own flourishing.

And yet I must confess that the historical events that brought my abbey into existence perplex and even disturb me. I simply fail to grasp the awful providence which allowed the ghastly and godless Communist party in Hungary to lay the initial tracks for my own priestly and monastic path. The logic is perfectly obvious to me: if there is no Communism in Hungary, then there is no suppression of Zirc; if Zirc is not suppressed, then there is no need for Cistercians to escape and seek shelter in America; if the Hungarian Cistercians do not come to America, then they establish no Cistercian Abbey in Dallas (and perhaps the creation of the University of Dallas, the initial reason for their choice of Dallas since they comprised half of the first faculty, does not come about); if there is no abbey, then there is no monastery for me to enter after I attend the University of Dallas. My life would be so entirely different had the Stalinist bastards not overrun Hungary after the Second World War.

Abbot Wendelin, am I supposed to be grateful for the agony that crushed so many souls, yet made possible my life as a monk wearing black and white? Should I not rightly feel a great remorse, a sort of spiritual survivor's guilt, at the fact that my own light was enkindled at the cost of so much torture for others, most of whom I never even met? As a math teacher, you might remind me that such rigorous and linear logic breaks down when applied to history, and that faith alone can perceive providence at work even in the midst of such wretchedness. You might also recall a phrase in one of your letters, rooted in your physics background, that "All matter is ultimately light." Your prayers may not have resulted in the conversion of the Communists who tortured you, but perhaps they are somehow converting the evils you endured into the light that my confreres and I are trying to spread and share with everyone we meet. Ultimately, I suppose that silence alone is a worthy response to such troubled thoughts; perhaps the quiet of my abbey church, so conducive to prayer, offers a touch of consolation this side of death's curtain.

When Fr. Lawrence's mortal remains were reinterred in the Zirc church in 2001, a tombstone was made to mark his resting place. The epitaph begins with Zechariah 13:7: "Strike the shepherd, and the sheep will be scattered." My Hungarian elders revere both you and Fr. Lawrence, and speak of you both as saints, and I do not doubt them in the slightest. They do not tell us, although it is a manifest fact to me, that my generation, all of us young American Cistercians, have a most noble heritage to boast of and uphold. Whereas I have come merely at the eleventh hour to the work of God's vineyard, you have already borne the burden of the day and the heat. Though I cannot hope to imitate your courage, I can at least resolve, with the help of your prayers, to live as a worthy son of so noble a father, to enkindle and enlighten all who come to me looking for the light of Christ, and to rejoice with you soon in the perpetual light of that eternal day for which I toil now.

Actually, you provided me with a solution to my inability to understand God's providence in your 1949 letter:

> Everyone must walk to the end of his own course. No matter how hard it appears, we should not be afraid of anything as long as we walk in the direction of God's will. So we too can give no other answer than the one Thomas gave, the disciple who liked to reason too much but proved always generous at the moment of decision: "Let us then go to die with him" (John 11:16).

Abbot Wendelin, I consider myself to be the Thomas you spoke of, and I pray that his words may be mine should I have the honor and burden of suffering, as you did, for love of our Lord.

Father Aloysius Kimecz, O.Cist.[1]

DEAR FATHER ALOYSIUS,

While digging recently in a desk drawer for something, I pulled out a notepad whose existence I had neglected for several years. On roughly thirty sheets of paper, I had penned a series of anecdotes and observations about you during my first years in the abbey. I cannot recall what prompted me to put these assorted highlights into writing. While I occasionally keep a journal of random reflections, this notepad is unique, in that it is devoted completely to your quips and quirks.

My discovery of the notepad coincides with another momentous event that concerns you quite directly. We living monks just finished building a crypt attached to the church. We exhumed your mortal remains and those of our other twenty-two confreres, and we brought them home to rest permanently on abbey soil. As a result of this great and unprecedented occasion in the life of our abbey, I have been thinking of you a great deal lately, and I thought you might enjoy hearing about a few of my written reminiscences in this letter. Perhaps they can act as the thank-you for your friendship during my first years in the monastery, a simple act of gratitude I never got to voice aloud in your presence. You passed away when I was studying in Rome, and I did not get to offer a proper goodbye to you this side of eternity.

I distinctly remember the first time we met. I was a novice, a newly recruited monk of three weeks or so, when the novice master told me to pick you up at the dentist's office. You had been secluded in your room that entire three-week period, so I did not know what you looked like. As soon as I pulled into the parking lot, I deduced that you must be the old

1. Father Aloysius Kimecz, O.Cist. (1926–2010) was a monk and priest of the Cistercian Abbey Our Lady of Dallas.

man standing on the curb. Though I had never seen your face, your disheveled clothes and manner of standing betrayed the typical Hungarian out-of-place-ness I had already recognized in other Cistercian confreres. You initiated a pleasant banter on the drive back to the abbey, and you concluded the ride with the gentle phrase, "I am happy that we will be friends."

So we had a positive start to our relationship, but several older monks had warned me that you were fickle in your friendships and subject to sudden mood swings and irrational, long-lasting grudges. Rumors reached my young ears of the disastrous time you "got sick" in the middle of the semester and had to go to a clinic for several years, but I did not allow them to dictate my impressions of you.

One of the great gifts of my novitiate was the opportunity to tend, medically and pastorally, to the needs of elder and frail confreres, such as Fr. Henry, Fr. Pascal, Fr. David, and yourself. The young brothers were enlisted as chauffeurs for scheduled trips to the doctor's office, as well as the hospital and pharmacy for impromptu necessities. I celebrated my first birthday as a monk by taking you to the emergency room and accompanying you for eight hours after you fell and gashed your hand open, exactly the wrong thing to have happen while on blood-thinning medication. I am not so holy as to say that I rejoiced to waste the day in service of this sort, but I do recall thinking that this experience would be a template for me moving forward in my monastic life. "This is just what monks do when their brother is in need," I put on the notepad after returning home, and I have not forgotten the lesson you involuntarily imparted to me that day.

Sometime during my novitiate, I was tasked with inserting your vast array of pills into the proper boxes for your weekly consumption. You were grateful for this service of mine, and it revealed a certain trust in me that you did not bestow willingly on other confreres. We soon established a routine on those evenings when I came to fill the pillboxes. I would sit at your desk, crowded with prescriptions and bottles without caps, fake flowers (which you occasionally watered) in pretty pots, and a steady stash of metallic cranberry juice cans. You would observe me in silence from your dark blue armchair nearby, legs elevated as always, and sometimes you would share an anecdote from your most recent trip to the latest doctor whom you considered an idiot. When I had finished the assembly process (which usually took from fifteen to twenty minutes, given the abundance of pills I had to work with), I would close the last lid triumphantly and say, "Okay, Father, you're good to go!" That would be your cue to say "Thank you," pause, and then proceed to a topic of conversation, usually about my studies or abbey life or some piece of mail that came for you that day.

In the course of those talks, I began to form a picture of you as a complete human being—not the broken old man whose mental frailty and swollen legs prevented him from taking part in most community activities, but the whole man, even if only visible in fragments. From the Hungarian Cistercian funneled from one prison camp to another after World War II, to the theology student in Rome (you called those "the happiest years of my life"), to the Spanish teacher at the University of Dallas and Form Master at our Cistercian Preparatory School, I gathered pieces of your life and quietly stored them, both on paper and in my own mind. I quickly came to understand that you had a mischievous sense of humor; you flashed a devious grin when you had a joke in mind, and many of your stories contained plentiful doses of comedy. My favorite has to be the time when Fr. Paul answered the abbey phone as a discerning college student. You were chatting with him at the reception desk, and grew so annoyed at the recurrent ringing of the phone that after the third call in five minutes, you picked up the phone, screamed, "Shut the hell up—we're trying to have a conversation here!" and slammed the receiver down! (Fr. Paul himself confirmed that story, down to the last detail; no word on how badly you scandalized the poor caller!)

When I entered the monastery, you were still able to move about independently when you felt well enough, and I personally witnessed your conniving pranks on hapless confreres. You knew that Fr. Roch had a breakfast tradition of pouring himself a glass of orange juice and leaving it unattended on the counter while returning the OJ to the fridge. I saw the scene unfold, slowly and inevitably, from my spot in the refectory: you waited until he deposited his glass of orange juice, "sprinted" to his glass, took the juice, and began to gulp it down. When Fr. Roch noticed that his poured glass was missing, he looked up and found you devilishly downing the glass, a huge smile creasing your face as you finished the fluid with a satisfied burp!

Aside from your clever shenanigans, you provided the community with gifts both tangible and intangible. I recall you depositing the laundry bag of individual monks at their doors as long as you were able to walk. I would sometimes catch you "in the act": the black bag hanging loosely from your hand (which naturally clammed shut on account of your blood clots), and that dear glimmer in your eye suggesting that you were pleased to be spotted doing some good deed, however small. I still proudly possess a picture you gave me of Filippino Lippi's famous *Apparition of the Virgin to Saint Bernard*. Upon closer inspection, I realized that you had cut the image from a postcard someone in Hungary sent you, and placed it in a small frame which you bent to make it hang on the wall. Several stains, perhaps from coffee spills, line the white edge of the postcard, but I don't mind in the slightest; it is a precious memento to me of your friendship.

Your presence, of course, mattered far more than any deed or gift you provided. We shared the same feast day party, given that our patron saints were celebrated on back-to-back days (Saint Aloysius Gonzaga on June 21, Saint Thomas More on June 22). The monks like to joke that we need to do a better job of spacing out our patron saints in order to secure more feast day parties and prevent joint celebrations, but I didn't mind sharing the patronal spotlight with you at all.

My fondest memory of you, however, is one that you surely never pondered. I always try to arrive in the church a bit before the community's morning prayer begins for some personal prayer time. I loved discerning a quiet rustling sound from the back of the church and slowly growing louder as its source approached the sanctuary. The sound was that of slippers gently scraping the carpeted side aisle. Given your blood clots and the terrible swelling of your legs and feet, you were not able to lift your feet, and your plastic-soled slippers conveyed you gently and deliberately, barely six inches per shuffled step, toward your seat in choir. Every time I heard those hobbled feet announce their quiet presence, I would smile and think to myself, "Father Aloysius has persevered another day."

And when you couldn't bring yourself down for the prayer hours, we took turns carrying food to your room, sometimes breakfast, lunch, and dinner. I remember your breakfast requests: toast with butter and jam, a banana, and two bottles of cranberry juice. After knocking twice at your door, I always let myself in before you answered. I learned to tell from the position of your blinds whether it was going to be a good day or "not a good day": open blinds allowing light to flood in meant that you were feeling well, closed blinds meant that you "were sick," and that some combination of kidneys, blood clots, and depression had the upper hand.

Father Aloysius, you mentioned once how you were in a dark place before the young batch of Americans began to populate the abbey in the 2000s, but that we brought treasured light to you by our presence and love. You would be the first to admit that you were not the easiest confrere to get along with, but I remain very grateful for the opportunity to befriend you and serve you. If we young monks lengthened your life by a few years, I think it is fair to say that the graces were mutually poured out on all of us.

Our new crypt allows us to put the original roots of our community back in the ground you and the others tilled for so many decades. Our proximity to your mortal remains, located on the side of the Abbey church, reminds us of the duty we the living must embrace: to persevere as you did in the Cistercian life, no matter the obstacles. It also gives us the reassurance that the bonds of monastic fraternity stretch across the divide of death, and permit us to await a great reunion in God's good time.

Galadriel[1]

To GALADRIEL, LADY OF Lórien,

I write to you, fair lady of the Elves, from the world of men, trusting that your dwelling place in the undying lands of Valinor has not removed the thought of us from your heart. What your eyes gaze upon in those blessed havens I do not know, but I have heard tell of what those eyes, whose depths reveal "the wells of deep memory," saw through many ages of Middle Earth. May it be granted to me one day to gaze into those eyes and to draw forth the fullness of light and wisdom which you now enjoy.

I am aware of the great esteem in which you are held, and not only by the race of men. You bestowed upon Gimli, the valiant dwarf, three strands of your golden hair; so great was his veneration of you that he boasted to his traveling companions that you were more precious than all the jewels under the earth, where his people dwell. Some mortals have argued that his dedication to you is reminiscent of the devotion of Catholics to Mary, the mother of Jesus. While I certainly acknowledge the similarities, I prefer to think of you more broadly as a symbol and dispenser of what Catholics call *grace*, the free and undeserved aid which comes to men from outside themselves as they seek after God. I cannot help but regard your encouragement to the fellowship of the ring, asserting that "hope remains" even in the midst of great evil, as precisely the help they needed in order to embolden their hearts and steel their resolve. Your gift of the light of Eärendil's star to Frodo, bestowed with the assurance that it would be a light to him in dark places "when all other lights go out," is a radiant image for grace.

It is in connection with your graceful intercession on behalf of the fellowship that I have pondered the meaning of one particular phrase that

1. Galadriel is an immortal Elven lady in J. R. R. Tolkien's series *The Lord of the Rings*. She encourages Frodo and the other members of the fellowship to destroy the Ring of Power.

came from your mouth. In the first book, you spoke of standing alongside Celeborn, Lord of the Galadhrim, for years uncounted. You noted that "together through ages of the world we have fought the long defeat."[2] You did not proceed to define what you meant by "the long defeat," and those words have captivated me by their obscurity and profound sadness. You and the Elves faced the unending challenge of withstanding the relentless approaches of shadow across Middle Earth, and your foresight permitted you to see the apparent triumph of the forces of evil. Such prescience must inevitably have produced in you a creeping despair, especially in view of the tragic calamity of Isildur and his fellow men, who wilted when presented with the chance to destroy the ring of power forever.

A friend recently asked me if I thought that our present civilization was falling, gradually and inexorably, into a dark abyss of political regress and cultural chaos. She had in mind the daily bombardment of terrifying news of atrocities all over the world, the specter of violence emerging in what previously had been peaceful cities in our homeland, and a widespread overthrow of moral precepts that can only be the fruit of a barbaric selfishness dominating the human heart. I immediately thought of "the long defeat" in this regard. Indeed, the temptation to a forlorn outlook for humanity is quite strong at present, even if fatalistic sorrow has been prominent in previous ages as well. The darkness of terrorism and shadows of hatred loom ever larger, especially as the races of men forget how to speak with one another, resorting instead to factious and tribal instincts, totally unhinged from principles of reason, virtue, and charity.

Worries of civilizational scope would be sufficient to bow the head of anyone, Elf or mortal. But men, unlike the Elves, carry the added burden of living while running toward the fixed finish line of death, without the possibility of stopping before they reach it. Each individual human being lives out a personal long defeat in this sense—no matter how optimistic or pessimistic the person may be, the end is the same. This mortal anguish is at the heart of all epic tales, for it frames all the accomplishments of men and paints them with a melancholic and shadowy hue.

But to return to you, Lady Galadriel, you did not permit "the long defeat" to conquer your heart, and another phrase of yours, "Yet hope remains," galvanized those fighting the power of Sauron. You are, in a very real sense, a tragic character in a great saga: you valiantly resist certain

2. Tolkien, *The Fellowship of the Ring*, 400. Most of the references and quotes in this letter come from book II, chapter 7, entitled "The Mirror of Galadriel."

doom on behalf of your people, yet eventual victory seems impossible given the imminence of awful defeat. What I have always wondered is this: what convinced you that hope yet remained, even when you could foresee the terrible consequences of the weakness of men and the consolidation of evil forces? What allowed you to trust the fate of Middle Earth to a collection of hobbits, men, elves, and dwarves, whose little victories and small steps seemed so innocuous to a great and wrathful power? A different but related question also arises: How were you able to "pass the test" when the one ring to rule them all was within your grasp, assuring yourself that you would indeed sail to Valinor?

Regardless of the courageous audacity men display in the face of death, their hearts are selfish, and infected with greed. (I will stop writing in the third person, for I am one of them.) We so easily convince ourselves that our own passion or intelligence alone can procure the glory and power we desire, and we fall prey to the illusion that our desires will be satisfied when such things are in our clutches. The virtues we are taught and then put into practice are meant to guard us from being overwhelmed by the desires that surge, often violently, within our hearts. If we believe that we alone act and direct the course of our lives by sheer force of will, and that nothing and no one ultimately accompanies us, we come to think only in terms of our own devices. However noble our sentiments and worthy our purpose, we deem ourselves and our own strength sufficient for the tasks at hand.

Elrond was right, however, when dismissing the possibility that men could destroy the ring, for men indeed are weak. He saw with his own eyes the abject failure of Isildur long ago in the caverns of Mount Doom, and the same scene is played out, though usually on a much smaller scale, in every mortal life. Our minds are poisoned by power, our wills corrupted by a mad selfishness, our noble intentions laid waste by wayward lusts for what we cannot have. A saint named Augustine once asked himself rhetorically, "Why do you rely on yourself, only to find yourself unreliable?"[3]

It is quite easy, I admit, to tend toward pessimism when gauging the affairs of human beings. But you did not yield to such pessimism, and your gracious help was exemplified most in the warm hope you planted in the hearts of the fellowship members when all seemed cold and lost. Your great symbol of hope, fair Lady of Light, was entrusted to Frodo, and I can think of no more beautiful or fitting description of grace than the light of Eärendil's star. You did not give him precise instructions on how to use it,

3. Augustine, *Confessions*, 151.

or when he would need to deploy it. You simply entrusted it to his care, and assured him that it would see him through the darkest passageway in his journey. And so, when all other lights had gone out for him in Shelob's Lair, when he was utterly alone, bereft by his own fault of his faithful Sam, he remembered your light, and it guided him when he needed it most.

Most importantly, your light was external to Frodo. It did not come from within him, and so it was not his own strength or brilliance which lighted his way. This lesson is repeated time and again in his agonizing journey to Mordor. With the unflagging assistance of Sam, the wizarding work of Gandalf, and the bravery shown by Aragorn to overcome his doubt and mortal weakness, the effort to destroy the ring was a collective one. Their quest and victory illustrate, I think, a most essential truth of human life: if men are rightly guided, or rather, if we allow ourselves to be guided rightly by the light of grace, there is hope that we will not perish from evil, whether within us or outside us.

Of course, even with your light, Galadriel, and even with the maximum amount of grace possible, the battle is far from easy. Men make their individual journeys difficult enough without a hostile enemy seeking their lives! But at least the knowledge that aid external to us is available, and even willingly dispensed, can give us the necessary confidence to turn our wills outward, to banish the cancers of fear and despairing pride which mix so potently in our feeble minds, and to channel what is noble and good in us to worthy ends.

The great creator of Middle Earth himself would probably abhor my allegorical reading of your character. He did, however, once offer an illuminating interpretation of your statement about "the long defeat." In a private letter to a woman named Amy Ronald, he explains that precisely on account of his Roman Catholic faith, he does not expect the history of mankind to be anything but a long defeat—"though it contains (and in a legend may contain more clearly and movingly) some samples or glimpses of final victory."[4] He was perfectly aware that this ephemeral existence is a vale of tears and cruel sorrow, having lived through two ghastly world wars, and he soberly admits that the overwhelming power of evil permits but a few stars to shimmer in the ever dimming dusk of history.

But he also declines to explain what final victory might look like. I myself do not expect to see anything remotely approaching an ultimate triumph in my precious few and fleeting days on earth. The work of final

---

4. Tolkien, *The Letters of J. R. R. Tolkien*, 255.

victory is truly beyond me—*and yet*, as the story of Frodo and the fellow-ship shows with utter clarity, it cannot happen without the contribution of individuals who cooperate with the grace bestowed, or even thrust, upon them. For your luminous example of grace and encouragement in the face of evil, Lady Galadriel, I thank you, and beg that you would continue to shed your kindly light upon my, and mankind's, humble endeavors.

Bibliography

Augustine. *Confessions.* Translated by Henry Chadwick. Oxford: Oxford University Press, 1992.

Benedict XVI. "Meeting with Representatives from the World of Culture" (September 2008). http://w2.vatican.va/content/benedict-xvi/en/speeches/2008/september/documents/hf_ben-xvi_spe_20080912_parigi-cultura.html.

————. "Meeting with the Representatives of British Society, including the Diplomatic Corps, Politicians, Academics, and Business Leaders" (September 2010). https://w2.vatican.va/content/benedict-xvi/en/speeches/2010/september/documents/hf_ben-xvi_spe_20100917_societa-civile.html.

Bernard of Clairvaux. *Five Books on Consideration: Advice to a Pope.* Cistercian Fathers 13. Kalamazoo, MI: Cistercian, 1976.

Birzer, Bradley B. *American Cicero: The Life of Charles Carroll.* Wilmington, DE: Intercollegiate Studies Institute, 2010.

Burtt, E.A., ed. *The Teachings of the Compassionate Buddha: Early Discourses, the Dhammapada, and Later Basic Writings.* New York: New American Library, 1955.

Chesterton, G. K. "A Turning Point in History." In *The Fame of Blessed Thomas More, Being Addresses Delivered in His Honour in Chelsea, July 1929,* 63–64. London: Sheed and Ward, 1929.

Dickens, Charles. *Great Expectations.* Oxford: Oxford University Press, 1993.

Eliot, T. S. *The Complete Poems and Plays, 1909–1950.* New York: Harcourt, Brace, and World, 1971.

Esposito, Thomas. *Letters of Fire.* New York: St. Pauls, 2015.

Froude, James A. *A History of England,* Vol. 2. London: Longmans, Green, 1872.

Fry, Timothy, ed. *RB 1980: The Rule of St. Benedict.* Collegeville, MN: Liturgical, 1981.

Gregory the Great. *Moralia in Iob.* Corpus Christianorum Series Latina 143. Turnhout, Belgium: Brepols, 1979.

Hart, Dolores, and Richard DeNeut. *The Ear of the Heart: An Actress' Journey from Hollywood to Holy Vows.* San Francisco: Ignatius, 2013.

Heaney, Seamus. "Digging." In *Poems, 1965–1975,* 3–4. New York: Farrar, Straus, and Giroux, 1980.

Heraclitus. *Fragments: The Collected Wisdom of Heraclitus.* Translated by Brooks Haxton. New York: Viking, 2001.

Justin Martyr. *The First and Second Apologies.* Translated by Leslie William Barnard. Ancient Christian Writers 56. New York: Paulist, 1997.

King, Martin Luther, Jr. *A Testament of Hope: The Essential Writings and Speeches of Martin Luther King, Jr.* San Francisco: Harper, 1991.

Lagerkvist, Pär. *Barabbas.* New York: Vintage, 1989.

Laurentin, René. *Bernadette of Lourdes: A Life Based on Authenticated Documents.* London: Darton, Longman, and Todd, 1998.

Leclercq, Jean. *The Love of Learning and the Desire for God: A Study of Monastic Culture.* 3rd ed. New York: Fordham University Press, 2001.

"Letter to Diognetus." In *Early Christian Fathers,* edited by Cyril C. Richardson, 218. New York: Touchstone, 1996.

MacIntyre, Alasdair. *After Virtue: A Study in Moral Theory.* 2nd ed. Notre Dame: University of Notre Dame Press, 1984.

Maraniss, David. *Clemente: The Passion and Grace of Baseball's Last Hero.* New York: Simon and Schuster, 2007.

More, Thomas. *A Dialogue Concerning Heresies.* The Complete Works of St. Thomas More 6. New Haven, CT: Yale University Press, 1981.

———. *The Sadness of Christ.* Princeton: Scepter, 1993.

Planned Parenthood of Southeastern PA v. Casey, 505 US 833 (1992). https://supreme.justia.com/cases/federal/us/505/833/case.html.

Plato. *The Republic of Plato.* Translated by Allan Bloom. 3rd ed. New York: Basic, 2016.

Pruit, Daniel. "Be Anxious for Nothing." *Striving to Inspire* (November 28, 2013). https://danielpruit/wordpress.com/author/dpruit.

Ratzinger, Joseph. "Homily for the Mass to Elect the Roman Pontiff." (April 18, 2005.) http://www.vatican.va/gpII/documents/homily-pro-eligendo-pontifice_20050418_en.html

Richardson, Cyril C., ed. *Early Christian Fathers.* New York: Touchstone, 1996.

Rogers, Carl R. *On Becoming a Person: A Therapist's View of Psychotherapy.* Boston: Houghton Mifflin, 1961.

Rogers, Elizabeth Frances, ed. *St. Thomas More: Selected Letters.* New Haven, CT: Yale University Press, 1961.

Seuss, Dr. *Oh, the Places You'll Go!* New York: Random House, 1990.

Shakespeare, William. *The Complete Works of Shakespeare.* London: Oxford University Press, 1942.

Sullivan, Andrew. "I Used to Be a Human Being." In *New York Magazine.* (September 19, 2016.) http://nymag.com/selectall/2016/09/andrew-sullivan-my-distraction-sickness-and-yours.html.

Tolkien, J. R. R. *The Letters of J. R. R. Tolkien.* Boston: Houghton Mifflin, 1981.

———. *The Lord of the Rings: The Fellowship of the Ring.* New York: Ballantine, 2012.

Wegemer, Gerard B. *Thomas More: A Portrait of Courage.* Princeton, NJ: Scepter, 1995.

Wegemer, Gerard B., and Stephen W. Smith, eds. *A Thomas More Source Book.* Washington, DC: Catholic University of America Press, 2004.

Werfel, Franz. *The Song of Bernadette.* San Francisco: Ignatius, 2006.